THE CONTOURS OF EUROPEAN ROMANTICISM

The Contours of European Romanticism

Lilian R. Furst

UNIVERSITY OF NEBRASKA PRESS

First published 1979 by
THE MACMILLAN PRESS LTD
London and Basingstoke

First published 1979 by
UNIVERSITY OF NEBRASKA PRESS

Library of Congress Cataloging in Publication Data

Furst, Lilian R
  The contours of European Romanticism.

  Includes Index.
  1. Romanticism – Europe.   2. European literature –
  History and criticism.   I. Title.
PN603.F76   809'.91'4   79–15141
ISBN 0–8032–1954–7

Printed in Great Britain

To my Father
in appreciation of his wisdom and tolerance

Willst du ins Unendliche schreiten,
Geh nur im Endlichen nach allen Seiten.

Willst du dich am Ganzen erquicken,
So musst du das Ganze im Kleinsten erblicken.
                                            Goethe

If you want to stride into the infinite,
Explore the finite in all directions.

If you want to delight in a vision of the Whole,
You must perceive the Whole in the smallest details.

Contents

Preface

The search for an understanding of European Romanticism has in itself come to assume some of the attributes of a Romantic quest. It tends to be infinite and progressive, to use the words with which Friedrich Schlegel chose to characterise Romantic poetry in his famous 116th *Athenäum* Fragment; but infinite and progressive not so much in the sense of a purposeful advance, as of an endless continuance. Like the quest for the Holy Grail, or Heinrich von Ofterdingen's aspiration towards the symbolic blue flower of his dream, the pursuit of Romanticism is inspired by the longing to grasp an elusive phenomenon; its existence is manifest, but definitive possession always seems to escape us. As long as fifty years ago, Paul van Tieghem, one of the pioneer comparatists in this field, lamented that 'le romantisme paraît de plus en plus un Protée, tantôt nuage et tantôt serpent' ('Romanticism appears increasingly Protean in form, at times a cloud, at others a serpent'). In that same 'Essai sur le romantisme européen' in the *Bibliothèque universelle et Revue de Genève* (ii (1929) 42–60), he went on to ask: 'Faut-il donc renoncer à s'entendre? Le romantisme européen restera-t-il un terme dépourvu de sens réel, en *eidôlon* vain?' ('Must we then give up hope of agreement? Will European Romanticism remain a term devoid of real meaning, a mere *eidôlon*?'—p. 43).

That is a question that has, in one guise or another, been asked repeatedly ever since, and because experience convinces us that Romanticism is no mere *eidôlon*, various answers have been offered since van Tieghem's time. He himself suggested that we should proceed by identifying the common characteristics of European Romanticism. He enumerated four aspects that he called 'negative', i.e. opposition to rationalism, absence of serene optimism, rejection of the dictates of French taste, and opposition to the classical tradition; and no fewer than thirteen 'positive' features: philosophical and religious preoccupations expressed with vehemence, the primary of feeling, individualism, freedom of the imagination, an abundance of imagery, an interest in the objective world of nature, exotic or historical local colour, an interest in national origins, the cult of originality, the importance of dream and mystery, the belief in the sacred seriousness of art, flexibility of form and freedom of style. But which of these seventeen features are we to adduce when we read that the poetry of T. S. Eliot, Allen Tate, A. R. Ammons or Philip Larkin is 'romantic'? How helpful in fact is the ant-heap approach, the painstaking accumulation of variegated components? Do they coalesce into an intergrated pattern of lasting validity? It has long become apparent that the old piecemeal method does not contain a solution to our recurrent problems in dealing with Romanticism, although it still has its adherents and emulators.

Ultimately one reaches the conclusion, I think, that European Romanticism is too large, too complex, and, above all, too elastic to be captured in some scholarly butterfly-net, pinned down and dissected at convenience, to be classified once and for all. It defies such an approach, not least because it is still alive and changing, in Protean manner. Its extraordinary capacity for continual evolution and renewed relevance is the mainspring of its importance, but it is also the source of our difficulties. We must recognise that Romanticism possesses in high degree the quality that Coleridge ascribed to beauty: 'multeïty in unity'. Its unity resides in its affirmation of the transcendental imagination as the fundamental means of perception and of expression; that is its normative centre of gravity. But this is a capacious concept which admits of an immense variety in the individuality of each poet. To try to simplify the exuberant diversity of Romanticism to some formulaic scheme is a reductive and misguided undertaking. Only by accepting and facing its multeïty, can we ever hope to do justice to Romanticism, let alone to live in tolerable peace with it.

This book, therefore, does not attempt to give a definition of Romanticism. It seeks instead to delineate its contours, to explore its sinuosities and to trace its lines of demarcation. The introductory essay posits three distinct, though closely interrelated senses of the word: the archetypal, the historical and the aesthetic. These are far from hard and fast categories. On the contrary, they represent three pliable concentric forms, whose contours can and do overlap at a number of points. It is around these three connotations of 'romantic' that the subsequent studies are grouped. Romantic irony and the Romantic hero illustrate primarily its archetypal signification, although in both cases the historical moment is also of considerable consequence, insofar as the archetype becomes dominant at a particular period. The three pieces that examine the processes of transmission attest to the intricacies of the historical movement. Finally, under the heading 'aesthetic', some of the later permutations of basic Romantic tendencies are followed beyond the bounds of its customary temporal limits.

These studies are based on material gathered over many years. Most of them have appeared previously in earlier versions. For the present volume I have, however, carried out extensive revisions. This was done in order to take into account not only recent criticism, but also the development of my own conception of Romanticism. For if it is the hallmark of Romantic poetry 'dass sie ewig nur werden, nie vollendet sein kann' ('that it is always evolving, never completed'), as Friedrich Schlegel would have it, then surely our thinking about Romanticism must show a readiness to partake in that same process of evolution, even if we can never attain the definity of completion. But therein lies the unending fascination of Romanticism.

L. R. F.
Cleveland, September 1978

Acknowledgements

An earlier version of 'The Contours of European Romanticism' under the title 'Further Discriminations of Romanticism' was written for *Neohelicon* (Budapest: Akadémiai Kiadó, & The Hague and Paris: Mouton), iii, No. 3–4 (1975) 9–26, and is included here by permission of the editors of that journal.

'The Romantic Hero, or is he an Anti-Hero?' was written for *Studies in the Literary Imagination* (Georgia State University), ix, No. 1 (Spring 1976) 53–67, to whom acknowledgement is herewith made.

'Mme. de Staël's *De L'Allemagne*: A Misleading Intermediary' first appeared in *Orbis Litterarum* (University of Odense), xxxi (1976) 43–58, and is reprinted here by permission of the editors of that journal.

'Benjamin Constant's *Wallstein*' was first published in *Romanistisches Jahrbuch* (Universität Hamburg), xv (1964) 141–59, and is included here by permission of the editors of that journal.

'Two Versions of Schiller's *Wallenstein*' was written for *Modern Miscellany presented to Eugène Vinaver*, ed. T. E. Lawrenson, F. E. Sutcliffe & G. F. A. Gadoffre (Manchester University Press, and New York: Barnes & Noble, 1969) pp. 65–78, and is included here by permission of Manchester University Press.

'Novalis' *Hymnen an die Nacht* and Nerval's *Aurélia*' was first published in *Comparative Literature* (University of Oregon), xxi, No. 1 (Winter 1969) 31–46, to whom acknowledgement is herewith made.

'The Configuration of Romantic Agony' was published under the title 'The Structure of Romantic Agony' in *Comparative Literature Studies*, x, No. 2 (June 1973) 125–38, and is included here by permission of the University of Illinois Press.

'Kafka and the Romantic Imagination' originally appeared in *MOSAIC: A Journal for the Comparative Study of Literature and*

Ideas, ii, No. 4 (July 1970) 81–9, published by the University of Manitoba Press, to whom acknowledgement is herewith made.

I should like also to record my gratitude to the endowment of the Flora Stone Mather Visiting Professorship at Case Western Reserve University, Cleveland for a grant of research funds towards the preparation of the manuscript.

1 The Contours of European Romanticism

It was Arthur O. Lovejoy who first suggested, in a well-known article published in 1924 ('On the Discrimination of Romanticisms'), 'that we should learn to use the word "Romanticism" in the plural'.[1] To discriminate between romanticisms would, he argued, 'clear up, or . . . diminish, this confusion of terminology and of thought which has for a century been the scandal of literary history and criticism' (p. 234). Almost a century before Lovejoy, Musset had already satirised that confusion in the serio-comical deliberations of Monsieur Dupuis and Monsieur Cotonet. Each month, with the arrival of the Parisian journals in their rural retreat at La-Ferté-sous-Jouarre, these innocent devotees of culture became more and more bewildered by that prominent and obviously fashionable term 'romantic'. Did it, they wonder, mean this? – or that? – or that? running through a whole gamut of possibilities, each sufficiently close to contemporary controversies to remain credible, yet sufficiently ludicrous to expose the absurdity of the entire discussion. Dupuis and Cotonet never find that absolute, final answer, for which they grope with such tenacity for years on end. Their fundamental error, like that of so many of their successors, lies in their pursuit of *the* single, ultimate definition that will provide the key to the understanding of Romanticism and that will, moreover, be valid for ever. It is this common, but mistaken assumption that was first seriously called into question by Lovejoy's article: that is its main importance. In its recognition of the plurality of romanticisms, it marks a vital turning-point in the history of the critical evaluation of European Romanticism.

Lovejoy's distinctions are, admittedly, quite conservative. In spite of his contention that 'the discrimination of the romanticisms which I have in mind is not solely or chiefly a division upon

1

lines of nationality or language' (p. 235), he first differentiates between 'a movement which began in Germany in the seventeen-nineties' and 'another movement which began pretty definitely in England in the seventeen-forties', and a third 'which began in France in 1801' (p. 235). Later on he does elaborate on the divergence in character between the German Romanticism of the 1790s and the English Romanticism of the 1740s. However, Lovejoy's examples, illuminating though they are in themselves, are all drawn from the eighteenth and early nineteenth centuries, i.e. from the time of the Romantic movements in literature and the arts. But the term is so frequently used of other periods too that it continues to engender that uncertainty that Lovejoy deplored and sought to remedy. In order to achieve his purpose of diminishing 'this confusion of terminology', we must, I believe, make broader and bolder discriminations than he did. If we are to grapple with the appearance of 'romantic' in relation to phenomena both long before and long after the accepted bounds of the historical movement, as we patently have to, we need some divisions that transcend outer historical limitations. My modest proposal is that we identify three separate, though closely interconnected, spheres of reference: the archetypal, the historical, and the aesthetic. These represent the major contour lines of European Romanticism.

The archetypal denotes the 'forever recurring emotional condition', as Henry H. H. Remak[2] has so aptly called it. Remak, like many other critics, categorically excludes consideration of this strand from his article on 'West European Romanticism' because his focus is on the literary movement of the later eighteenth and of the nineteenth century. But no attempt to chart the contours of Romanticism can ignore its existence. As a constant modal temper, it has for one of its cardinal features a quintessential independence of time and place. To acknowledge this at the outset immediately helps to dispel and obviate certain of the difficulties attendant on the usage of 'romantic'. For instance, it removes the grounds for Lovejoy's surprise that H. C. J. Grierson[3] should have referred to Plato as 'the first great romantic';[4] that astonishment reflects Lovejoy's too exclusive linking of the notion 'romantic' to a specific period. The actual appropriateness of the term to Plato or to any other writer or thinker of the Classical Age is open to question. What must be recognised, however, is the validity of 'romantic' as an archetypal concept. Once this is done, it may be applied at any period and in any setting to any individual bearing its marks, irrespective of connections to the literary movement known as Romanticism.

There is no more cogent phrase to characterise the archetypal romantic than that with which Virgil in the *Aeneid* (Book VI, line 314) described the dead awaiting passage across the Styx in Charon's ferry, stretching out their hands 'ripae ulterioris amore' ('with love for the yonder bank'). The romantic by temperament is always intuitively drawn by a yearning for the yonder bank. The contrast with the realist's sober, sensible contentment with the blessings of this bank is well brought out in Goethe's ballad *Adler und Taube* (Eagle and Dove). A young eagle with a broken wing lands in a grove of myrtle-trees, a pleasant spot with shade, warmth, a stream, soft moss, and golden sand. But to the eagle, to be earth-bound is tantamount to death; he longs to soar on high, and derives little comfort from the well-meant advice of the dove who chances on him as he frets at his limitations. After enumerating the advantages of life in the myrtle-grove, the dove concludes:

> O Freund, das wahre Glück
> Ist die Genügsamkeit,
> Und die Genügsamkeit
> Hat überall genug.

> (Oh friend, true happiness
> Lies in contentedness,
> And contentedness
> Is everywhere content.)

To which the eagle can only reply:

> O Weise, sprach der Adler, und tief ernst
> Versinkt er tiefer in sich selbst,
> O Weisheit! Du redst wie eine Taube!

> (How wise, said the eagle, and deep in thought
> He sinks deeper into himself,
> Oh wisdom! you speak like a dove!)

This little fable has implications far beyond its immediate relevance to Goethe's autobiographical self-portrayal as an eagle straining to escape the confines of Frankfurt's bourgeois society. It summarises, in a brilliant miniature, the polarity between the archetypal realist and the archetypal romantic: the dove with his sagacious, pragmatic enjoyment of the here and now, as against the eagle with his longing for a way of life less comfortable perhaps than his present state, but incomparably more exciting.

Such yearning for the inaccessible is the hallmark of the romantic temperament. It springs largely from the idealisation of all that is beyond reach; the very fact of its inaccessibility indeed greatly heightens its potential attractiveness. Frequently, though not invariably, the yearning is associated with motifs familiar from the old tales of romance; it may be a love object, or glory in combat, or the thrill of adventure, or some dream of life either in the past (or future), or in a remote part of the world, that is invested with the attributes of perfection.

The romantic's intrinsic urge to transcend the confines of his existence may unleash dynamic energies. Of this the prototype is Goethe's Faust, whose ethos of perpetual striving is a variation of the romantic's innate yearning. Conversely, the romantic's vague longings may prove destructive. Witness the case of Emma Bovary who resembles the eagle in her spurning of the one man with any genuine affection for her: her pathetic husband, Charles. Though her tastes may have been perverted by the spiritual diet of her adolescence, by the sentimental 'keepsakes' she cherishes, by her reading of *Paul et Virginie* and the novels of Scott, her appetite for these fantasies so remote from her rural, middle-class background, is in itself an indication of her inherent temperament. Emma is indefatigable in her pursuit of her mirage: 'Elle se promettait continuellement, pour son prochain voyage, une félicité profonde'[5] ('She kept on promising herself immense happiness on her next expedition'); only at length, when she 'retrouvait dans l'adultère toutes les platitudes du mariage' ('came in adultery upon all the platitudes of marriage' – p. 269), does she ask herself: 'D'où venait donc cette insuffisance de la vie, cette pourriture instantanée des choses où elle s'appuyait?' ('What was the source of this shortfall of life, this immediate rotting of all the things to which she turned?' – p. 263). She does eventually pose that crucial question, but she cannot answer it. Significantly, Flaubert follows that question-mark with suspension points ('. . .') as if to invite an answer from the reader who must first and foremost point to Emma's constitutional disposition: that of the romantic entranced by a vision and impelled by the urge to seek it out. In its striking delineation of the archetypally romantic personality lies one of the greatnesses of *Madame Bovary*.

Once the existence of such an archetypal romanticism without allegiance to period or locale is posited, certain problems of literary classification are more readily overcome. For example, it is with equal reluctance that one includes Hölderlin among the *Romantiker* or excludes him. His poetry shows distinct romantic traits, notably in his aspiration towards the ideal. But this should be recognised for what it is: an expression of archetypal romanticism, rather than an affiliation to any one school. The same holds true of poets more remote temporally from the nineteenth-century Romantic movement, such as Tasso, or Yeats with his Celtic ideology. It could indeed be argued that no major poet is without some degree of this kind of romanticism. The so-called Hellenism of several nineteenth-century poets, which has puzzled many critics, could also be regarded as a manifestation of this archetypal phenomenon. And it is an exploitation of our latent yearning for romance that leads to the marketing of perfumes, lingerie and holiday places under that magically evocative adjective, 'romantic'. There is obviously a streak in human nature that is strongly drawn to a primordial romanticism of this sort.

The correlation of this archetypal romanticism with the historical romanticism of the late eighteenth and early nineteenth centuries is like that between the endemic and the epidemic. The comparison with the demographic outbreak of a disease is not intended as a value judgement, but merely as a quantitative measure. The archetypal romanticism that had always existed as a sporadic human trait became the dominant mode at the turn of the eighteenth century. It was – to a greater or lesser degree, according to local circumstances – systematised into a number of artistic movements. It grew and spread in both extent and complexity, but it still remains an entity whose contours can be traced. At this point, Lovejoy seems to be overstating his insistence on confusion when he maintains that:

When a man is asked, as I have had the honor of being asked, to discuss Romanticism, it is impossible to know what ideas or tendencies he is to talk about, when they are supposed to have flourished, or in whom they are supposed to be chiefly exemplified.[6]

Let us take Lovejoy's strictures one by one. First, 'when they were supposed to have flourished': whatever other controversies surround historical romanticism, there is a wide measure of agreement on its timing; the European Romantic movement was at its zenith in the closing decade of the eighteenth century and the first thirty or so years of the nineteenth century. The exact dates vary from country to country, depending on the retarding or impelling effect of local conditions. Remak[7] cites the 1790s to 1830s for Germany, 1800 to 1843 for France, 1780 to the 1830s for England, 1830–1845 for Spain, and 1816 to the 1850s for Italy. The position is perhaps not quite so simple, as I shall go on to suggest later, but by and large these are generally accepted time-spans for historical romanticism.

The second of Lovejoy's objections concerns the identity of the Romantics: 'in whom they are supposed to have been chiefly exemplified'. In this area, the approach has undergone considerable refinement in recent years, above all in the refutation of the earlier simplistic categories that had been the product of positivistic scholarship which often sought to label poets like chemicals in a laboratory. C. H. Herford's divisions, for instance, in *The Age of Wordsworth* now seem facile:

> English poetry in the age of Wordsworth had three characteristic haunts. It throve in seclusion among the mountain glens of England, in society among her historic Borderlands, and in exile beyond the Alps. Stowey and Grasmere, Tweedside and Ettrick, Venice and Rome, were the scene of potential activities as alien as the places, and yet all embodying some element of the Romantic revival.[8]

The first, the Wordsworth group, was said to comprise Wordsworth, Coleridge, Bowles, Crabbe, Bloomfield, Clare and Elliot; the second, the Scott group, consisted of Scott, Campbell, Moore, Southey, Leyden, Hogg, Cunningham, Motherwell, Rogers , Keble, J. Montgomery, Heber, Milman and Mrs Hemans; while the third, the Shelley group, was made up of Byron, Shelley, Keats, Landor, Tennant, Frere, Horace Smith, Wells, Wade, Darley and Procter. The sheer incongruity of this assortment of major and miniscule poets illustrates the artificiality of such a method. Later classifications into the 'Lake School' and the 'Satanic School' are hardly more helpful. All of them, remarkably, omit any reference to Blake. Such synthetic arrangements have been superseded by the appreciation of each poet's individual voice; but there can be no reasonable doubt as to the identification of the English Romantics.

In France the contours have usually been drawn by generation. In the volume devoted to Romanticism in the standard history of French literature, Pierre Moreau[9] singles out first 'La Génération de René' which includes, alongside Chateaubriand, Mme de Staël, Ballanche, Joubert, Constant, and Joseph de Maistre. Then comes the period of the *Cénacle*: Hugo, Vigny, Lamartine, Nodier, Lamennais, Barante, and Augustin Thierry; and finally, 'Le Romantisme de 1830', composed of many of the writers associated with the *Cénacle* with the addition of Musset and, somewhat later, George Sand and Nerval. Again, the overlapping from one to the other underlines the unreliability of such generational slicing. Division of the French Romantics according to their political alignment or religious beliefs into Liberals, Royalists, Catholics, etc. is even less satisfactory because of the rapid shifts of opinion. Here, too, the old static compartmentalisation is giving way to a greater flexibility that grows from an awareness of the dynamic developmental flow of literature.

Only in Germany does the traditional split into two major groups have any real validity. There was certainly a continuity, both personal and ideological, between the *Frühromantik* (the Early Romantics) and the *Hochromantik* (the High Romantics), but the differences are great enough to warrant a distinction. In many fundamental respects the interests of the two generations were at variance. The *Frühromantiker*, with their marked predilection for the metaphysical, focused their attention mainly on the transcendental and on the mediation of their mystical perception of the infinite. The *Hochromantiker*, by contrast, less speculative and more practical, concentrated on the creation of the *Märchen* (wondrous tales) and *Lieder* (songs) for which German Romanticism is best known. Moreover, while the *Frühromantiker* were cosmopolitan in outlook, the *Hochromantiker* inclined increasingly to a fervent patriotic nationalism. Nevertheless, in none of these literatures, nor in those of Spain, Italy and other European countries, should Lovejoy have encountered any serious dilemmas in identifying the Romantics in the historical sense.

His third heading, 'what ideas or tendencies', is indeed a thornier matter, but even here a consensus of opinion has been reached. The definitive statement of the cardinal unitary features of European Romanticism, given by René Wellek in his essay, 'The Concept of Romanticism in Literary History', has been widely endorsed:

> If we examine the characteristics of the actual literature which called itself or was called 'romantic' all over the continent, we find throughout Europe the same conception of poetry and of the workings and nature of the poetic imagination, the same conception of nature and its relation to man, and basically the same poetic style, with a use of imagery, symbolism, and myth which is clearly distinct from that of eighteenth-century neoclassicism.[10]

To these basic tenets a variety of features may be added, and some modifications made. Morse Peckham, for instance, in his attempt to lessen the conflict he perceived between Lovejoy's plea for discrimination and Wellek's synthesising tendencies, suggested the following amendment:

> What then is Romanticism? Whether philosophic, theologic, or aesthetic, it is the revolution in the European mind against thinking in terms of static mechanism and the redirection of the mind to thinking in terms of dynamic organicism. Its values are change, imperfection, growth, diversity, the creative imagination, the unconscious.[11]

To prove much the same point, Henry H. H. Remak[12] has evolved his own method, a schematic catalogue of the prime qualities of European Romanticism with an assessment of their relative force in Germany, France, England, Italy and Spain. These are the characteristics he lists as yard-sticks: imaginativeness, cult of strong emotions, restlessness and boundlessness, individualism, subjectivism, introversion, cult of originality, interest in nature, greater emphasis on religion, mysticism, *Weltschmerz,* liberalism, cosmopolitanism, nationalism, interest in folklore and primitivism, medievalism, anti-neoclassicism, interest in Nordic mythology, supremacy of lyrical moods and forms, historical drama and novel, reawakening of national epic, greater flexibility of form, irony, vagueness, symbolism, rhetoric, exoticism, and realism in local colour. Needless to say, not all these traits of Romanticism are present in each national movement. Remak's tables are studded with such qualifying phrases as 'but', 'less strong', 'within limits', 'relatively', 'not primary', 'notable exceptions' and so on. These indicate the perceptible fluctuations in the strength of the various features in different countries, as well as some dissimilarity in the forms they assumed, determined as they were by local circumstances and native traditions.[13] But such national differences can only be established on the basis of an acknowledgement of the fundamental common elements of historical Romanticism. This is, to invert Coleridge's terms, unity in multeïty. The recognition of its homogeneity as a movement throughout Europe is perhaps the most important advance in the comparative approach to Romanticism since Lovejoy's day. The doubts that he harboured in 1924 as to 'what ideas and tendencies' were meant, have to a large extent been dispelled in the past fifty years.

Not entirely, however. The demarcation of historical Romanticism still poses some problems, foremost among them that raised originally by Lovejoy himself in his discrimination between the two major strands of Romanticism. He summarised the contrast as follows:

> Between the assertion of the superiority of 'nature' over conscious 'art' and that of the superiority of conscious art over mere 'nature'; between a way of thinking of which primitivism is of the essence and one of which the idea of perpetual self-transcendence is of the essence; between a fundamental preference for simplicity – even though a 'wild' simplicity – and a fundamental preference for diversity and complexity.[14]

As an example of the first type of Romanticism Lovejoy cites Joseph Warton's *The Enthusiast*, written in 1740; for the second he refers to the theories of the *Frühromantik* in the 1790s. The objections to Lovejoy's argument are fairly obvious: the fifty-year interval separating his two examples, during which the nascent Romanticism of the 1740s underwent further evolution, not to say, a mutation; the unfortunate imbalance inherent in the comparison of a rather second-rate poem with a complicated aesthetic theory; and the fact that Warton's *Enthusiast* belongs, ideologically as well as temporally, to Pre-romanticism, which differs in several vital respects from the Romantic movement that it foreshadows. Nonetheless, in spite of these reservations, Lovejoy's thesis is of great importance. Two currents do clearly run side by side in historical Romanticism: the naturalistic whose prime emphasis was on naturalness, primitivism and simplicity; and the transcendental which stressed the superiority of conscious art, and showed a preference for diversity and complexity, to use Lovejoy's apt terms. To the former belong not only Pre-romanticism, and notably the *Sturm und Drang* (Storm and Stress) of the 1770s, but also a number of the English poets: Wordsworth, Clare, Crabbe, possibly Keats. The outstanding expression of the naturalistic strain during the period of historical Romanticism comes, however, in the French Romantic movement. The *romantisme* of the early years of the nineteenth century plainly bears the marks associated with the first type of Romanticism. Its preference for naturalness, primitivism and simplicity are best understood as part of the revolt against all that Neoclassicism had represented: artificiality, over-refinement, and arabesques of convention. The impact of Rousseau's writings with their advocacy of a return to nature in the widest sense reinforced its rebellious tendencies. As a result, French *romantisme* has more in common with the *Sturm und Drang* than with the *Frühromantik*. On the other hand, a striking affinity of ideals, aims and idiom links the *Frühromantik* to the French poets of the later half of the nineteenth century from Nerval and Baudelaire onwards through the French Symbolists.[15] They, together with Coleridge, Blake and Shelley, pertain to the second, the transcendental direction of Romanticism. There are good grounds for maintaining, as Albert Béguin[16] and some of his successors have done, that it was only with this later wave of poets that the second type of Romanticism came to play a vital part in France. Be that as it may, Lovejoy's thesis of two Romanticisms cuts across the comfortable periodisation that sites historical Romanticism neatly between 1790 and 1830. In order to include the earlier manifestations of naturalistic Romanticism as well as the later expressions of transcendentalism, the dates would have to be extended to, at least, 1740–1895.

While the contours of archetypal romanticism follow a stable course along steady lines, those of historical Romanticism are of a conspicuous, though by no means unchartable sinuosity. But this sinuosity in the contours of historical Romanticism leads to some blurring of the silhouette at this point. For if the *terminus a quo* of historical Romanticism is none too easy to determine with any assurance, the *terminus ad quem* is even more perplexing. The very diversity that is universally conceded to be one of the salient features of historical Romanticism has fostered a beguiling and hazardous elasticity in the use of the term.

'Romantic' recurs in literary and artistic criticism with stubborn persistence and generally with little or no attempt at a designation of its precise meaning. Let me refer back to the examples I cited in the preface: two major recent collections of poems, *Sphere* by A. R. Ammons, and *High Windows* by Philip Larkin, were enthusiastically hailed as 'romantic',[17] and in another recent review-article the word was applied with equal liberality to T. S. Eliot, Hart Crane, Allen Tate, Whitman and Wallace Stevens.[18] This is not a matter of careless misuse, yet there is a disturbing vagueness in such usage. The implication would seem to be that these poets were writing within a tradition represented by their predecessors in the historical Romantic movement. These examples offer in fact a significant pointer to what has become a common assumption: the existence of a third dimension to the term 'romantic', distinct from the archetypal or the historical connotations, namely as a broad aesthetic concept. As such it has long become part of the critical vocabulary of our day. In meaning it is patently indebted to the archetypal and the historical alike, from which it derives its main thrust, though it lacks the relative explicitness of either. That is at one and the same time its strength and its weakness; its breadth of reference increases its usefulness, though its want of specificity detracts from its force. Its convenience as a portmanteau term all too easily exposes it to over-use and abuse.

How then are the contours of this third sense of 'romantic' to be traced? One possibility is to envisage them as an outer perimeter to historical Romanticism. The development from the historical to the aesthetic is then considered as a process of expansion into ever widening circles. Jacques Barzun chose the image of a river when he wrote: 'romanticism does not die out in 1850 but branches out under different names like a delta'.[19] Another of his favourite images, that of the family, is particularly illuminating in this context if the transition from the historical to the aesthetic sense of 'romantic' is likened to the growth of the nuclear into the extended family. In essentials the features of the far-flung family echo and repeat those of the original nucleus, but with varying degrees of intensity. Thus as a general aesthetic term 'romantic' continues to signify the primacy of the individual consciousness, an emphasis on emotion rather than reason, the espousal of irrationalism rather than rationalism, the reliance on vision rather than the orientation to reality, the trust in subjective reactions rather than objective standards, obedience to the dictates of an inner, rather than an outer imperative of order. Perhaps the most appropriate succinct definition of this aesthetic connotation of 'romantic' is that which Rémy de Gourmont coined for Symbolism: 'une littérature très individualiste, très idéaliste, au sens strictement philosophique du mot, et dont la variété et la liberté mêmes doivent correspondre à des visions personnelles du monde'[20] ('a literature that is highly individualistic, highly idealistic in the philosophical sense of the word, and whose very variations and freedoms reflect, of necessity, personal visions of the world').

Although Rémy de Gourmont intended to characterise only Symbolism, his phrases have a significance beyond his original purpose. The contour lines are freely drawn here, with a generous sweep. For in its aesthetic sense, 'romantic' surpasses the limits of any specific movement or movements to denote one of the basic directions of art. Ultimately it betokens that imaginative transfiguration that is the opposite of the mimetic imitation called 'realistic'. Those are the two contrary poles. If the realist leads us through the honest gates of horn, as Harry Levin[21] has taught us, the romantic takes us through the extravagant gates of ivory, the portals of dreams, illusions and fantasies – of horror as well as of beauty. When 'romantic' in the aesthetic sense is interpreted in this way as a basic tendency, it obviously has some relation to the archetypal meaning. But whereas the archetypal manifestations of romanticism are not subject to temporal or spatial demarcations, those of aesthetic romanticism do, in practice, follow on the historical movement, from which they derive. The artistic modes of aesthetic romanticism devolve from the matrix of historical romanticism; they reflect the momentous changes in manner and style that resulted from the enthronement of the subjective imagination as the prime source of perception and creativity. Thus it is the literary and artistic schools of the late nineteenth and early twentieth centuries that are the best examples of the romantic in this third connotation.

Symbolism is clearly romantic, and indeed in a dual sense, sited as it is in that area where the contours of the historical and the aesthetic run closest to each other. Its direct descent from historical romanticism is evident in the Symbolists' striking affinity to the German *Frühromantiker*. The two groups share many basic ideals and techniques: the underlying belief in transcendental idealism and in the metaphysical nature of art; the conception of the artist as a visionary prophet and mediator of the infinite; the quasi-religious and magical aura surrounding creativity; the paramount role of the symbolic image as the vehicle for the expression of the inexpressible; the tendency to modify traditional forms in an experimental search for new means more fitted to the presentation of the ineffable vision. So intimately is Symbolism connected to historical Romanticism that it is tempting to regard it as a final, grandiose wave of that sprawling movement, just as the *Sturm und Drang* may be considered a preliminary flood of the tide. Through its filiation to historical Romanticism on the one hand, and on the other, its prefiguration of subsequent poetic modes, Symbolism stands at a crucial point of transition. Its aesthetics represent a heavy contour line on the map of modern literature.

While Symbolism is at the convergence of the contour lines, Impressionism is already in the outer, the aesthetic perimeter. The Impressionists have – quite wrongly – been taken for realists because they painted directly from nature. Yet their purpose was far from the faithful reproduction of reality. The subject as such was of minor importance to them, a pretext more than a topic. What mattered was the perception of the subject; to borrow Zola's famous phrase, it was 'un coin de la nature vu à travers un tempérament'[22] ('a corner of nature seen through a temperament'), through a certain individual pair of eyes. For this reason the Impressionists would happily paint the same scenes over and over again, the same apparently mundane hay-stacks, the same water-lilies, the same cathedral front. The repetition of the same held a particular fascination for them insofar as the object would appear different at different times of day or year, under different illumination. And it was the recording of this subjective view that was their paramount aim. Their painting is essentially visionary, imaginative and personal, and must therefore stand in the lineage of Romanticism.

This holds true of Surrealism too, though it departs in some respects from the Romantic paradigm, particularly in its rejection of mysticism and in its attachment to this earth. But its main tenets point to its origins in the Romantic tradition: the primacy of the free-wheeling imagination, released from any restraints of logic; the conviction that the true essence of being can best be revealed through art; the leading role of the irrationally inspired mind in a poetic state open to Orphic insights; the flexibility of artistic forms; the belief in the actuality of a 'féerie intérieure' ('an inner realm of the wondrous'), as André Breton[23] called it. These are the characteristics that justify the use of the term 'romantic' in its third, aesthetic sense, in relation to Surrealism.

Expressionism offers yet another variant. Like Surrealism, it has certain deviant distinguishing features, such as its concern for the typical rather than the individual, the shrill stridency of its tone, and that tendency to inflation that was to lead towards the grotesque. However, in its opposition to naturalistic mimeticism as well as to automatism; in its emphasis on inner vision, on the creative powers and on the imagination; in its intense subjectivity; in the importance it attached to the almost autonomous image; in its championship of the supremacy of the artist as creator, as the passionate centre of a dynamic vortex; in its frequent mingling of the arts: in all these attributes Expressionism appears as yet another recrudescence of the romantic in its wider, aesthetic signification.

There is no need to multiply these examples any further, or to list instances of the occurence of 'romantic' in recent literary and artistic criticism. The word and the idea obviously continue to flourish long after the demise of the Romantic movements of the late eighteenth and early nineteenth centuries. Its repeated usage can be understood only if its existence as a broad aesthetic concept is accepted in addition to its specifically historical – and archetypal – sense.

To use the term 'Romanticism' in the plural, as Lovejoy urged, and to discriminate between its varied manifestations: between the timbre of the national historical movements, between their successive waves, and between its differing connotations outside its historical boundaries – such discriminations are the starting-point for a truer understanding of European Romanticism. But this understanding does not lead to fixities and definities; rather, it is conducive of an appreciation of the character, potentialities, and also the problems inherent in Romanticism. Its kernel lies in change, growth and development, for Romanticism is essentially dynamic and organicist. As van Tieghem[24] suspected, it is Protean, and it may well be comparable – as he thought – to a serpent in its dangerous windings, but it is not cloud-like. Its contours can be charted, even though the map will never attain a diagrammatic neatness. And at those very points where the contours crowd together most closely, where the lines converge in the densest configuration. Romanticism can be seen in its richest – and often perplexing – abundance.

NOTES TO CHAPTER 1

1. *Publications of the Modern Language Association of America*, xxxix (1924) 229–53; reprinted in amplified form in A. O. Lovejoy, *Essays in the History of Ideas* (Baltimore: Johns Hopkins Univ. Press, 1948) p. 235. All subsequent references are to this edition.
2. Henry H. H. Remak, 'West European Romanticism: Definition and Scope', in *Comparative Literature: Method and Perspective*, ed. Horst Frenz & Newton P. Stallknecht (Carbondale, Ill.: Southern Illinois Univ. Press, 1961) p. 225.
3. Herbert J. C. Grierson, 'Classical and Romantic', in *The Background of English Literature* (London: Chatto & Windus, 1925) pp. 256–90.
4. Lovejoy, *Essays in the History of Ideas*, p. 229.
5. Gustave Flaubert, *Madame Bovary* (Paris: Garnier, 1961) p. 262. All subsequent references are to this edition.
6. Lovejoy, *Essays in the History of Ideas*, p. 232.
7. Remak, 'West European Romanticism', pp. 238–9.
8. C. H. Herford, *The Age of Wordsworth* (London: Bell, 1897) p. 146.
9. Pierre Moreau, *Le Romantisme* (Paris: Duca, 1957).
10. René Wellek, 'The Concept of Romanticism in Literary History', in *Concepts of Criticism*, ed. Stephen G. Nichols, Jr. (New Haven and London: Yale Univ. Press, 1963) pp. 160–61.
11. Morse Peckham, 'Toward a Theory of Romanticism', *Publications of the Modern Language Association of America*, lxvi/i (1951) 14.
12. Remak, 'West European Romanticism', pp. 238–45.
13. See Lilian R. Furst, *Romanticism in Perspective* (London: Macmillan, 1969, and New York: Humanities Press, 1970).
14. Lovejoy, *Essays in the History of Ideas*, p. 244.
15. See Lilian R. Furst, *Counterparts: The Dynamics of Franco-German Literary Relationships, 1770–1895* (London: Methuen, and Detroit: Wayne State Univ. Press, 1977) pp. 99–173.
16. Albert Béguin, *L'Âme romantique et le rêve* (Paris: Corti, 1939).

17. Calvin Bedient in *New York Sunday Times*, 22 December 1974, and 12 January 1975.
18. Harold Bloom in *New York Sunday Times*, 5 February 1978.
19. Jacques Barzun, *Classic, Romantic, and Modern* (New York: Doubleday, 1961) p. 99.
20. Rémy de Gourmont, *Promenades littéraires*, 3rd ed. (Paris: Mercure de France, 1912) vol. iv, p. 82.
21. Harry Levin, *The Gates of Horn. A Study of Five French Realists* (New York: Oxford Univ. Press, 1963). The epigraph, taken from Homer's *Odyssey* (xix, lines 560–565), reads as follows in Robert Fitzgerald's translation:

> Two gates for ghostly dreams there are: one gateway
> of honest horn, and one of ivory.
> Issuing by the ivory gate are dreams
> of glimmering illusion, fantasies,
> but those that come through solid polished horn
> may be borne out, if mortals only know them.

22. Emile Zola, *Le Roman expérimental* (Paris: Fasquelle, 1923) p. 111.
23. André Breton, *Qu'est-ce que le surréalisme?* (Brussels: Henriquez, 1934) p. 24.
24. Paul van Tieghem, 'Essai sur le romantisme européen', *Bibliothèque universelle et Revue de Genève*, ii (1929) 43.

2 Romantic Irony and Narrative Stance

As long ago as 1808, in the *Vorwort zur Farbenlehre*, Goethe was already reluctant to use the term 'irony'; he introduced it with the qualifying phrase: 'um uns eines gewagten Wortes zu bedienen'[1] ('to use a hazardous word'). As recently as 1974, Wayne C. Booth, in the Preface to *A Rhetoric of Irony* (Chicago: Chicago University Press), still warned us that irony is a murky subject (p. xi). And when this hazardous and murky term 'irony' is allied to that equally hazardous and murky one, 'romantic', the meaning becomes even more enigmatic.

The difficulty stems not so much from any dearth of definitions as from the confusing multiplicity of interpretations that have been given to the phrase. Is romantic irony in fact a wholly independent, distinctive phenomenon, or is it a variant of 'ordinary' irony? Trustworthy critics assert each view with like authority: 'The first discovery one makes about Romantic Irony, . . . is that it has nothing to do with any simple conventional concept of Romanticism or with ordinary satiric or comic irony'.[2] That must be weighed against the opposing contention, that romantic irony is 'merely a more subtle and urbane manifestation of irony in the commonly understood sense, not something more glaring, eccentric or one-sided'.[3] Is it helpful to distinguish between 'subjective' and 'objective' irony, as Raymond Immerwahr has tried to do,[4] or are these highly confusing formulations ('hochst verwirrende Prägungen') in the words of Ernst Behler[5] who prefers to set romantic irony off against 'classical' irony and 'tragic' irony. If romantic irony is a category unto itself, are its lines of demarcation primarily historical, or modal? Are we to accept the common assumption that romantic irony began during the Romantic period, and that Friedrich Schlegel was its 'father'? Or should not its anterior manifestations in the works of Cervantes, Sterne and Diderot be examined? Where and how does romantic irony fit into the structures outlined by recent critics? D. C. Muecke,[6] for instance, has categorised irony into three 'grades' ('overt', 'covert', and 'private') and four 'modes' ('impersonal', 'self-disparaging', 'ingénu', and 'dramatised'); Wayne C. Booth[7] differentiates between 'stable' and 'unstable', 'covert' and 'overt', 'local' and 'infinite'. Yet neither of these leading scholars in the field of general irony makes any serious attempt to integrate romantic irony into his classifications. Muecke considers it as a thing apart, to which he devotes a separate section of his book,[8] while Booth evades the issue with no more than a few passing references to this thorny topic.

Apart from the inherent complexity of the subject, there is a fundamental methodological problem that bedevils any discussion of romantic irony. It can best be described as the danger of putting the cart before the horse, or even more drastically, of deciding which is the cart and which is the horse. The normal procedure would be to start with a definition of the matter under consideration. But what definition should be adopted in this instance? The most prevalent is that of Friedrich Schlegel: 'Ironie ist klares Bewusstsein der ewigen Agilität, des unendlich vollen Chaos.'[9] ('Irony is the clear consciousness of eternal agility, of the infinite fullness of chaos'.) The objections to this definition are manifold: its ultimate validity is open to question in the light of Schlegel's modifications and shifts of emphasis in his subsequent writings; its meaning is far from clear, as is shown by the plethora of often conflicting exegesis[10] that it has spawned; and its practical usefulness as a basis for concrete literary analysis is severely limited by its grandiose abstractness.

Under these circumstances, the only viable approach would seem to be a pragmatic one: an examination of the ironies in various texts with the aim of drawing certain conclusions about the workings of irony and, specifically, about the relationship of romantic irony to other kinds of irony. Yet irony is peculiarly hard to pinpoint, not only because it is by nature a form of disguise, but also because of its innate subjectivity. As a mode of perception, its arena is that crucial space between the narrator and the narrative on the one hand, and on the other, between the narrative and the reader. Thus, like beauty, irony may lie in the mind of the perceiver; ironies that strike one reader may wholly escape another. However, in the attitudes of the narrator to his narrative the presence of irony can be established with greater objectivity from the evidence of the text. Narrative stance is, therefore, a good base from which to explore ironies. The narrator's position vis-à-vis his narrative is indicative of his underlying stance; and the variations in that stance in turn reveal differing kinds and degrees of irony.

*   *   *   *   *

Traditionally the ironist has a dual vision, for he sees a latent reality divergent from the masking appearance on the surface. While recognising the incongruities of a situation, he seems to accept things at their face value. But at the same time, by one means or another, he lets his other view shimmer through, so that the reader too becomes aware of the alternative. In the reader's agreeing comprehension of the double meaning there is a tacit communication of the ironic perspective from the narrator to the reader.

A classic example of such irony occurs in the opening sentence of *Pride and Prejudice*: 'It is a truth universally acknowledged, that a single man in possession of a good fortune, must be in want of a wife.' At first sight this looks innocent enough, a direct enunciation not merely of a fact but of 'a truth universally acknowledged'. That phrase seems designed to lull the reader into a sense of security; it is a disincentive to doubt or question what is accepted by common consensus. Each of the three words, 'truth', 'universal', and 'acknowledged', contains an absolute affirmation, and together they suggest the existence of a firm moral basis for the society portrayed. However, the astute reader need not go very far into the novel to suspect the discrepancy between the manifest words and their intended meaning. He need not witness at length the manoeuvres of the young women and their mothers to ensnare a husband in order to grasp the potential for reversing that opening sentence to apply to a single woman – whether in possession of a good fortune or not – being in want of a husband. Still on that first page, Jane Austen has provided an unmistakable clue in the conversation between Mr and Mrs Bennet when Bingley's name is introduced with the comment: 'A single man of large fortune; four or five thousand a year. What a fine thing for our girls!' What is at stake evidently is not whether Bingley, being in possession of a good fortune, is in want of a wife – which may, or may not be the case – but that the Bennet daughters, especially since they are not in possession of any fortune, are much in want of husbands. The irony is discreet and covert; its place is behind the characters' backs, so to speak, above and outside the narrative. The narrator's stance is impersonal and detached; she functions as an extraneous observer of the story, gently uncovering its ironic undercurrents which the reader is intended to notice, but which are not forced on his attention.

A parallel though somewhat more complex example of the methods of an ironist with an impersonal stance occurs in George Eliot's *Middlemarch* in the passage that records Casaubon's feelings during his engagement to Dorothea (Book I, chapter 7):

Mr Casaubon, as might be expected, spent a great deal of his time at the Grange in these weeks, and the hindrance which courtship occasioned to the progress of his great work – the Key to all Mythologies – naturally made him look forward the more eagerly to the happy termination of courtship. But he had deliberately incurred the hindrance, having made up his mind that it was now time for him to adorn his life with the graces of female companionship, to irradiate the gloom which fatigue was apt to hang over the intervals of studious labour with the play of female fancy, and to secure in this, his culminating age, the solace of female tendance for his declining years. Hence he determined to abandon himself to the stream of feeling, and perhaps was surprised to find what an exceedingly shallow rill it was. As in droughty regions baptism by immersion could only be performed symbolically, so Mr Casaubon found that sprinkling was the utmost approach to a plunge which his stream would afford him; and he concluded that the poets had much exaggerated the force of masculine passion. Nevertheless, he observed with pleasure that Miss Brooke showed an ardent submissive affection which promised to fulfil his most agreeable previsions of marriage. It had once or twice crossed his mind that possibly there was some deficiency in Dorothea to account for the moderation of his abandonment; but he was unable to discern the deficiency, or to figure to himself a woman who would have pleased him better; so that there was clearly no reason to fall back upon but the exaggerations of human tradition.

This could be read as a straightforward account of the situation from Casaubon's point of view. While he speculates on the possibility of 'some deficiency' in Dorothea, there is little hint here that the deficiency might lie in him. That does not come into Casaubon's mind, but it does strike the reader because George Eliot has already carefully prepared us for the implicit irony. In the preceding twenty pages, the reader has been given ample warning of Casaubon's dry and sterile nature before the 'shallow rill' imagery of this passage. Brooke, speaking to his niece of her suitor (chapter 4), bluntly says: 'I never got anything out of him – any ideas, you know'; Mrs Cadwallader and Celia are scathingly sceptical of the 'great soul' with which Dorothea credits her future husband (chapter 6); and his letter of proposal (chapter 5) with its insistence on the 'need in my own life' and 'your eminent and perhaps exclusive fitness to supply that need' is a skillfully managed revelation of his monstrous self-centredness. When George Eliot adds: 'How can it occur to her to examine the letter, to look at it critically as a profession of love?', she in fact spurs the reader to do just that, to examine the letter critically. By the time we read that account of Casaubon's feelings during the engagement, we have sufficient insight into his personality to appreciate its hidden irony. We can, to use Wayne Booth's phraseology, 'reconstruct' its implied meaning, i.e. the deficiency in Casaubon, behind the voiced word, i.e. the putative deficiency in Dorothea. Here, as in the opening of *Pride and Prejudice*, all the features of 'stable irony'[11] are clearly visible: it is intended; it is covert, that is, intended to be reconstructed with meanings different from those on the surface; it is stable and fixed insofar as there is no further demolition of the reconstructed meaning; and it is finite in application. In such irony the author, though maintaining his aesthetic distance, is secretly in collusion with the reader. The reader comprehends what is between the lines (that is a part of his pleasure in reading this type of irony); more important, he understands and subscribes to the standards of judgement that underlie the irony. In this sense, the extraneous ironist who adopts an impersonal stance not only produces stable, reconstructible irony; he is himself the product and reflection of a society so confident of its values that it can rely on a community of opinion, on 'truth universally acknowledged'. Even where the 'truth' is not quite what it seems, the fundamental unity of opinion between narrator and reader persists, as does the basic certainty.

Not all ironies from an impersonal stance are as transparent or reconstructible with such definity as those of *Pride and Prejudice* and *Middlemarch*. In *Madame Bovary*, for instance, Flaubert made a great point of maintaining his objectivity as a narrator. His irony, in keeping with his proclaimed detachment, comes from outside and is always at the expense of the characters. In relation to the secondary characters it is stable and one-dimensional: Bournisien's absorption in cows that have wind to the exclusion of pastoral care for a troubled soul; Rodolphe's hypocritical farewell letter to Emma with its faked tear stains; Homais' Legion of Honour: all these ironies are so explicit as to verge on satire. But in regard to the main characters, Charles and particularly Emma, the position is much more complicated. Our ironic dual vision does, of course, note the incongruity between appearance and reality, between aspiration and limitation. Yet we are at intervals, certainly with Emma, tempted towards an empathy that is antithetical to irony. The source of this ambivalence may well lie in Flaubert's own difficulty in upholding his aesthetic distance throughout. The fluctuations in Flaubert's irony towards his central figure have beeen examined by Benjamin F. Bart in an illuminating article entitled 'Art, Energy, and Aesthetic Distance'.[12] Through an analysis of the changes that Flaubert made in his constant re-workings of his manuscript, changes of phrasing and of tense as well as more substantial textual revisions, Bart shows Flaubert's deliberate strategies to increase the aesthetic distance between himself, Emma and the reader. Especially in the section (Book I, chapter 6) about her reading and the dreams it inspires, 'Flaubert provokes a cool evaluation by not distracting our attention from the visions to her', for his artistry informs him that 'by giving her emotions directly, instead of confining us to her imaginings alone, the bitter irony implicit in the passage would have been diminished'.[13] Flaubert's ironic commentary on Emma is ultimately in the indirect, tacit, implicit mode characteristic of the ironist who manipulates his narrative from without, from an impersonal stance.

$$\star \quad \star \quad \star \quad \star \quad \star$$

But apart from this traditional, almost stealthy irony there is quite another kind that flamboyantly flaunts its irreverent unconventionality. Take the beginning of Diderot's *Jacques le fataliste et son maître*:

> Comment s'étaient-ils rencontrés? Par hasard, comme tout le monde. Comment s'appelaient-ils? Que vous importe? D'où venaient-ils? Du lieu le plus prochain. Où allaient-ils? Est-ce que l'on sait où l'on va? Que disaient-ils? Le maître ne disait rien; et Jacques disait que son capitaine disait que tout ce qui nous arrive de bien et de mal ici-bas était écrit là-haut.

> (How had they met? By chance, like everyone else. What were they called? Does it matter? From where were they coming? From the nearest place. Where were they going? Does one know where one is going? What were they saying? The master was saying nothing; and Jacques was saying that his captain said that all the good and the evil that befell us down here have been written up there.)

This startlingly idiosyncratic overture with its jagged surface, its provocative self-consciousness, its teasing perplexities and its stubborn refusal of any commitment, is far removed indeed from the sedate, impassive axiom that introduces *Pride and Prejudice*. The same shock effect that emanates from Diderot's questions strikes us again in Byron's abrupt declaration in the first stanza of the first Canto of *Don Juan*: 'I want a hero' –

> Most epic poets plunge 'in medias res'
>   (Horace makes this the heroic turnpike road),
> And then your hero tells, whene'er you please,
>   What went before – by way of episode,
> While seated after dinner at his ease,
>   Beside his mistress in some soft abode,
> Palace, or garden, paradise, or cavern,
> Which serves the happy couple for a tavern.

> That is the usual method, but not mine –
>   My way is to begin with the beginning;
> The regularity of my design
>   Forbids all wandering as the worst of sinning,
> And therefore I shall open with a line
>   (Although it cost me half an hour in spinning)

Narrating somewhat of Don Juan's father.
And also of his mother, if you'd rather.
                                    (stanzas vi and vii)

This is not the kind of invocation we expect in an epic; the poet should presumably, like Jane Austen, have done the thinking and arranging, the searching and agonising before beginning to write, presenting us then with the calm results instead of confronting us with his doubts and deliberations within his work. The romantic ironist does not, however, conform to the normal narrative expectations. The problems of creativity are very much in the forefront of his writing, even when they are more integrated into the narrative, as in E. T. A. Hoffman's *Kater Murr*. The bizarre genesis of this double tale, that literally runs the memoirs of the cat Murr into fragments of the biography of the musician Kreisler, is, so to speak, explained in the editor's foreword:

> Nach sorgfältigster Nachforschung und Erkundigung erfuhr der Herausgeber endlich folgendes. Als der Kater Murr seine Lebensansichten schrieb, zerriss er ohne Umstände ein gedrucktes Buch, das or bei seinem Herrn vorfand, und verbrauchte die Blätter harmlos teils zur Unterlage, teils zum Löschen. Diese Blätter blieben im Manuskript und – wurden, als zu demselben gehörig, aus Versehen mit abgedruckt!

> (After the most painstaking research and enquiry the editor finally ascertained the following: When the cat Murr was writing his memoirs, he casually tore up a printed book that he found in his master's house and used the pages without heed partly as an underpad and partly as a blotter. These pages remained in the manuscript – and were printed with it by mistake!)

The ensuing narrative is dislocated by impromptu switches from one tale to the other in mid-sentence with the barest abbreviated signs in parentheses to indicate which of the two is being told.

In all these instances, as in Sterne's *Tristram Shandy*, Pushkin's *Eugene Onegin* and Brentano's *Godwi*, the relationship between the author and his work, and also between the work and the reader, is totally different from that in Jane Austen, George Eliot or Flaubert. The actual creative process becomes so essential a part of the work that it often seems to usurp the centre of interest. Far from retreating behind his narrative, as Flaubert was at such pains to do, the narrator openly stands beside his story, ebulliently charting its progress. The impersonal, objective chronicler has been replaced by 'the self-conscious narrator who intrudes into his novel to comment on himself as a writer, and on his book, not simply as a series of events with moral implications, but as a created literary product'.[14] Wayne Booth's characterisation of the self-conscious narrator in comic fiction is singularly appropriate to the romantic ironist. His unremitting consciousness of himself is one of his cardinal characteristics. It is no coincidence that the term *Bewusstsein* (consciousness) recurs repeatedly as a key concept in the German theory of romantic irony. Friedrich Schlegel envisaged 'klares Bewusstsein'[15] ('clear consciousness') as the ironist's starting-point. Solger taught that: 'Die echte Ironie setzt das höchste Bewusstsein voraus, vermöge dessen der menschliche Geist sich über den Gegensatz und die Einheit der Idee und Wirklichkeit klar ist.'[16] ('True irony presupposes the highest degree of consciousness, whereby the human spirit attains clarity about the polarity and the harmony of idea and reality.') Likewise Adam Müller used the word alongside 'freedom' and 'irony' as if they were virtually synonymous: 'bist du mit Freiheit, mit Bewusstsein, mit Ironie von der einen Seite der Menschheit, von der *tragischen*, auf die andere, die *komische* Seite hinübergetreten?'[17] ('have you, with freedom, with consciousness, with irony, crossed from the one side of human life, the *tragic*, to the other, the *comic*?') Once his consciousness of himself as an artist becomes his archimedean point, the narrator can no longer commit himself without reserve to his creation, let alone disappear behind it. He is always aware not just of himself as an artist, but also of his work as an artifact.

Here an important differentiation must be made between the comic narrator and the romantic ironist: the comic narrator's consciousness centres on himself as a narrator, so that his purported bumblings are exploited for jocular purposes; the romantic ironist's consciousness, on the other hand, pivots on his work, so that the act of creation tends to become the subject of his writing. This emphasis conforms to Friedrich Schlegel's prescription that art should 'in jeder ihrer Darstellungen sich selbst mit darstellen' ('in each of its representations represent itself too'), or even more plainly, that it should portray 'auch das Producierende mit dem Produkt' ('also the productive process with the product') in 'künstlerischen Reflexion und schönen Selbstbespiegelung'[18] ('artistic reflection and beautiful self-mirroring'). Through the artist's self-consciousness, his constant observation of himself in the creative process, he maintains a degree of self-detachment that acts as a corrective to an excessively emotional subjectivity, and that forms the basis for his irony.[19] But this romantic irony is of a specific kind, for it is turned inward on itself, on to the actual creation of the work. Hence, romantic irony is in effect, as Ingrid Strohschneider-Kors repeatedly insists, 'Mittel der Selbstrepräsentation der Kunst'[20] ('means for the self-representation of art'). The narrator's stance is that of the self-conscious raconteur, standing alongside his narrative, offering overt comment on his work, voicing his views unabashedly in front of his characters, whose fate often appears of lesser importance to him than his own reflections.

The romantic ironist, therefore, assumes a prominence in his narrative that is the antithesis of the half-hidden, reticent position associated with the traditional ironist. Whereas the narrative, the thing created, is the focus of interest in *Pride and Prejudice*, *Middlemarch* or *Madame Bovary*, it is, on the contrary, the narration itself which incessantly attracts our attention in *Jacques le fataliste*, *Don Juan* or *Kater Murr*. The narrator holds the centre of the stage, disposing his characters and arranging his materials before our very eyes so that we see not the finished product, but the creative process. This incorporation of the creative process into the work is an outcome of the Romantic artist's conception of himself as a God-like figure, endowed with the divine power to shape and re-shape the world. When the narrator interrupts the narrative to reflect on its progress, he is not merely indulging in a playful whim, though it may well appear so at times. At a deeper level, he is asserting his freedom, the superiority of the God-artist over his work. He is the Prometheus fashioning a realm of the imagination at his own will. This is what Friedrich Schlegel had in mind when he affirmed 'Willkür'[21] ('caprice') as the poet's supreme faculty, and when he posited that 'Ironie ist eigentlich das höchste Gut und der Mittelpunkt der Menschheit'[22] ('irony is indeed the summit and centre of mankind'). In the context of the Romantic vision of the artist, irony is the sign of his total freedom, his right to manipulate, to destroy as well as to create.

This tension between 'Selbstschöpfung und Selbstvernichtung'[23] ('self-creation and self-destruction') is fundamental to the romantic concept of irony. In practice, it becomes manifest in the habitual breaking of the illusion which is generally considered one of the hallmarks of romantic irony. But this feature, more than any other, is liable to erroneous interpretation when the *pars* is mistaken *pro toto*, or when the effect is regarded as the cause. The breaking of the illusion with a particular ulterior purpose is, indeed, a prominent feature of romantic irony. However, this does not mean that every writer who has made play with the double level of art is a romantic ironist. From Aristophanes to Evelyn Waugh, from Chaucer to Aldous Huxley, a whole gamut of authors have broken the dramatic illusion, as Muecke has pointed out.[24] He goes on to suggest that such 'a reminder to his public (not necessarily an explicit one) that what they have before them is only a painting, a play, or a novel and not the reality it purports to be'[25] should rather be called 'proto-romantic' irony. The impetus for such proto-romantic irony might be described as negative, since its purpose is a reduction of the work of art from autonomous standing to its proper place in the scheme of the universe as 'only a painting, a play, or a novel'. On the other hand, in true romantic irony the breaking of the illusion is positive in intent, for it aims to demonstrate the artist's elevation over his work, his transcendence even of his own creation.

Whether such transcendence is accomplished or not is a moot point. Critics are agreed on the paucity of works that actually fulfil the theoretical programme for romantic irony; that most thorough scholar, Ingrid Strohschneider-Kors, deems only E. T. A. Hoffman's *Prinzessin Brambilla* to be wholly successful. If romantic irony is indeed a balance between self-creation and self-destruction, it may well be that the self-destructive aspects outweigh the self-creative ones. This is, obviously, contrary to intention, but the negative conclusion is borne out by the effects of romantic irony on the reader, by his reaction to the narrative stance adopted.

That stance is an introverted one. The romantic ironist, as we have seen, turns his gaze inwards on to the work he is creating and on to himself *qua* creator. Romantic irony is, thus, sited primarily between the author and his work; the reader, even when he is specifically addressed, is no more than an audience of the creative spectacle at best, and at worst merely an eavesdropper. There is none of that tacit rapport between author and reader that characterises the irony of Jane Austen and George Eliot, who convey their true opinions of characters and situations in oblique suggestions. The self-conscious romantic ironist, by contrast, makes his comments aloud; he has an active, an audible and visible role in his narrative but – ironically – in spite of his vociferous presence, his connection to his reader is tenuous because his orientation is towards himself and his work. This stance results in a crucial alteration in the whole narrative set-up. The buffer zone – what Heimrich calls the 'Indifferenzpunkt'[26] ('point of indifference') – between narrator and reader has to all intents and purposes been abolished, and with it the reader's sense of certainty vis-à-vis the work. The signals that he catches from the mercurial narrator may be loud and manifold, but they are inevitably conflicting and confusing as the narrator himself has no clear and firm position. He stands beside his work, making it, chopping and changing it, improvising or seeming to improvise, launching out in various directions only to retreat again. Although the lack of authorial control may be largely illusory, as far as the reader is concerned it appears very real, because the fiction of non-control is established with greater definity than anything else. The problems of interpretation, of reconstructing the intended meaning, become acute at this juncture, as we move from the stability of traditional irony, operating from its fixed and secure vantage point, to the instability of romantic irony that is riddled with ambiguities.

Ambiguity is, of course, an element of traditional irony too, but it is a directed ambiguity, limited in extent and intelligible to the reader so that it becomes a part of the multi-level communicative network that is irony. When we first read *Pride and Prejudice*, we may not know quite how to interpret the opening sentence, only suspecting an ulterior meaning behind the innocent surface; but by the time we have finished the novel, we do know how to interpret it. This is not the case with romantic irony where the unresolved ambiguities lead us progressively into a dizzying hall of mirrors. The interminable questions of the narrator in *Jacques le fataliste* – questions addressed to Jacques, to his master, to the reader, or just rhetorical questions – illustrate the way in which the romantic ironist throws the reader into a chaos of contingencies:

Mais, pour Dieu, me dites-vous, où allaient-ils? ... Mais,
pour Dieu, lecteur, vous répondrai-je, est-ce que l'on sait où
l'on va? Et vous, où allez-vous? Faut-il que je vous rappelle
l'aventure d'Ésope? Son maître Xantippe lui dit un soir d'été
ou d'hiver, car les Grecs se baignaient dans toutes les saisons:
'Ésope, va au bain; s'il y a peu de monde nous nous baignerons
....' Ésope part. Chemin faisant il rencontre la patrouille
d'Athènes. 'Où vas-tu? – Où je vais? répond Ésope, je n'en sais
rien. – Tu n'en sais rien? marche en prison. – Eh bien! reprit
Ésope, ne l'avais-je pas bien dit que je ne savais où j'allais? je
voulais aller au bain et voilà que je vais en prison...' Jacques
suivait son maître comme vous le vôtre; son maître suivait le
sien comme Jacques le suivait. – Mais, qui était le maître de
Jacques? – Bon! est-ce qu'on manque de maître dans ce
monde? Le maître de Jacques en avait cent pour un, comme
vous. Mais parmi tant de maîtres du maître de Jacques il fallait
qu'il n'y en eût pas un bon, car d'un jour à l'autre il en
changeait. – Il était homme. – Homme passionné comme
vous, lecteur; homme curieux, comme vous, lecteur; homme
importun comme vous, lecteur; homme questionneur,
comme vous, lecteur. – Et pourquoi questionnait-il? – Belle
question! Il questionnait pour apprendre et pour redire comme
vous, lecteur...[27]

(But for God's sake, tell me where they were going? .... But
for God's sake, reader, I'll reply, does one know where one is
going? You, for instance, do you know where you are going?
Must I remind you of Aesop's adventure? His master Xantippe
said to him one evening, in summer or in winter, for the
Greeks used to bathe at all seasons: 'Aesop, go to the baths; if
there are not many people, we will bathe...' Aesop leaves.
On the way he encounters the Athenian patrol. 'Where are you
going? – Where am I going? replies Aesop, I don't know. –
You don't know? straight to prison. – Oh well! answered
Aesop, didn't I say that I didn't know where I was going? I
wanted to go to the baths, and here I am going to prison...'
Jacques was following his master just as you follow yours; his
master followed his own just as Jacques followed him. – But
who was the master of Jacques' master? – Now, does one ever
lack a master in this world? Jacques' master had a hundred

more, just like you. But among so many masters of Jaques'
master there could not have been a single good one, for he
would change from day to day. – He was a man. – An
impassioned man, like you reader; a curious man, like you,
reader; an importunate man, like you, reader; a questioning
man, like you, reader. – And why was he asking questions? –
That's a good question? He was asking questions to learn and
to repeat, just like you, reader . . .)

In this whirling movement the narrator has in fact abdicated
responsibility for the world he is portraying; he makes no
pretensions at understanding it, let alone guiding us through it;
instead he stands there before us, beside his narrative, pondering
aloud how to proceed, and what to make of the story he is telling.

There is a cardinal difference here between the traditional and
the romantic ironist. It is implied in Wayne Booth's distinction
between Fielding's narrator in *Tom Jones* and Sterne's in *Tristram
Shandy*: 'the total impression derived from the instrusions of
Fielding's narrator is that he knows where he is going, whereas
Tristram otstensibly does not'.[28] Similarly, George Eliot knows
what she thinks of Casaubon, and so we too know what to think
of him. But we do not know what to think of Julien Sorel in *Le
Rouge et le Noir*, nor does Stendhal know, nor for that matter
does Julien know what to think of himself. As a narrator
Stendhal eschews the stance of omniscient certainty to explore
most brilliantly the opportunities for improvisation. In place of
the steady perspective that buttresses *Middlemarch*, we have in *Le
Rouge et le Noir* a shifting perspectivism that opens up potentialities but that precludes definitive interpretation or, in the
terminology of irony, easy reconstruction and finite application.
In the final analysis, the effect of romantic irony is disorienting.
Disorientation is, indeed, quintessential to romantic irony in that
it reflects a world dominated not by order, but by paradox. And
paradox, according to Friedrich Schlegel, finds its literary form
in irony: 'Ironie ist die Form des Paradoxen'[29] ('Irony is the
formal expression of the paradoxical'). Amidst all the questions,
the contradictions and the vexatory mirror images of romantic
irony, the only unequivocal affirmation, significantly, is of
paradox.

The disorientation is literally embodied in the form of the
narration. It becomes manifest in all those bewildering strategies

that disrupt the expected narrative process: the authorial intrusions, the breaks in illusion, the teasing questions, the interpolation of extraneous material, the jumbling of several strands, the temporal disjointedness, the literary allusions, the exchanges with a hypothetical reader, the comments on the comments, etc. In *Tristram Shandy, Jacques le fataliste, Don Juan, Kater Murr* and *Prinzessin Brambilla*, the apparatus of self-conscious narration dislocates the very structure of the narrative. So a far-reaching mutation occurs as the focus shifts from content to manner, from the narrative to the act of narration: the linear plot is replaced by the associative arabesque. These works fulfil Friedrich Schlegel's ideal: 'Gedichte, die durchgängig im Ganzen und überall den göttlichen Hauch der Ironie atmen.'[30] ('Poems that are filled with the divine breath of irony everywhere throughout their entire being.') In these works irony is all-pervasive; far from being a mere rhetorical device, it is the expression of a philosophical vision that recognises the world as paradoxical, and that seeks somehow to come to terms with its incongruities. Standing as he does beside his narrative, the romantic ironist is, at one and the same time, trying to master his recalcitrant material, yet also avowing its confusion. The supremacy of the impersonal ironist – supremacy over his universe as well as over his narrative – is not within the reach of the romantic ironist. Though he still grasps for it, he is *de facto* resigned to its loss.

★   ★   ★   ★   ★

There is still a third possible stance for the ironic narrator: it occurs when the authorial ironist withdraws completely to create characters who ironise themselves. As a separate recognisable voice, and as an extraneous point of reference, the author-narrator disappears, or at most remains in embryonic form, as in Dostoyevsky's brief comments at the opening and at the end of *Notes from Underground*, or in the psychiatrist's preface in Svevo's *Confessions of Zeno* (although the psychiatrist is himself, in fact, already a fictional persona). Sometimes the author-narrator is present just long enough to place the character in front of us before retreating behind his own creation. In *Herzog*, for example, Saul Bellow begins by sketching the figure of Herzog, giving us a fair amount of information about his physical location and his past; but when it comes to Herzog's present problems, the narrative responsibility gradually and almost imperceptibly shifts from the narrator on to Herzog himself, an inveterate self-analyst, whose confessions spill out into his compulsive letter-writing. With the atrophy of the outer narrator the narration is handed to the persona himself who tells his own story, generally in a first-person narrative, a diary or a stream-of-consciousness record. As a result, the reader has no objective view of the character, none of those well-placed clues to interpretation that George Eliot set out in her presentation of Casaubon. Instead, the reader is left unaided in direct confrontation with the persona's own, perhaps eccentric, and very likely unreliable self-perception.

Such internalisation of the narrative posture has important consequences for the ironist's stance. In this configuration, which is most common in post-Romantic fiction, but which does also occur earlier (e.g. *Tristram Shandy*), the irony arises within the economy of the narrative and is part of its immanent *Weltanschauung*. The narrator's situation is the opposite to that of the impersonal ironist, who stands above and outside his story, which he arranges for our convenient understanding. Nor is there even, as with the romantic ironist, a commenting narrator alongside the narrative – however confusing his commentary may at times be. In this third stance, when the ironist is placed within the narrative, the customary distance between the practitioner of irony and the object of his irony is obliterated, as the observer and the observed are telescoped into a single identity. This change has ramifications that go far beyond the technicalities of narrative perspective. It entails, in effect, a deviation of the entire perceptual perspective. Kierkegaard grasped this, and also its ulterior implications, when he criticised irony for its negation of historical actuality in favour of a self-created actuality that is the product of an overwrought subjectivity.[31]

The workings of overwrought subjectivity become apparent as the task of self-creation and self-destruction (Friedrich Schlegel's 'Selbstschöpfung und Selbstvernichtung'), previously the prerogative of the author-narrator, is passed to the protagonist-narrator, who builds and demolishes his own successive, or at times simultaneous roles. Joseph, in Saul Bellow's *Dangling Man*, projects his alter ego in the Spirit of Alternatives, *Tu As Raison Aussi*. Svevo's Zeno appears as the family failure, the typical anti-hero so devoid of will-power that he can never decide on any course of action, be it the renunciation of smoking or the choice of a career; yet he is also the family hero when he saves the family's honour and fortune, put in jeopardy by the reputedly successful Guido, who collapses into bankruptcy and suicide. Which of the two, indeed, is the success, and which is the failure? The self-image cultivated by Dostoyevsky's Underground Man is even more tantalisingly vexatory: is he really mean, sickly, unattractive, a social outcast, a mouse, a louse, a fly, a liar, as he goes on telling us; or is he, as he occasionally reassures himself, a highly civilised, sophisticated and intelligent being far more perspicacious than the mediocrities who surround him? We can never know, partly because he himself does not know; he has, like Zeno and Herzog, become the victim of his own irony, and so in fact do we. For when the narration is wholly from the viewpoint of an ironist–protagonist, the reader is deprived of the means whereby to correct or adjust the persona's self-vision by outer reference. Instead of being allowed to share the disengagement of the critical observer (as in *Pride and Prejudice*), he has no choice but to be sucked into the victim's swirling inner space. So we are plunged into the persona's paradoxes, ambivalences, ironies and schizophrenic dualisms without any prospect of escape to *terra firma*. From this hall of mirroring contradictions, there is not the exit to which a reliable narrator could lead us. And if the romantic ironist was an unreliable guide, compared to a Jane Austen or a George Eliot, at least he was still there, teasingly wending his way in and out of the narrative. Whereas with this third ironic stance, we are left to founder in shifting quicksands as the mobility of romantic irony quickens into a kinesis of uncertainties. Once the discriminating eye of the external narrator is eliminated, and with it his sure judgement, there is no longer any vantage-point – at least within the narrative – from which to organise experience and establish definities. The sense of disorientation, generated already by romantic irony, is intensified at this stage into an intuition of cosmic chaos. And just as the narrative strategies of romantic irony were a direct reflection of its stance, so here too, the derangement is graphically represented in the marked preference for labyrinths, for montage, for circular involutions, for the grotesque, for the ironisation of the fictional irony, for parody and self-parody.

In its infinite demolition, this is an unstable, continuously escalating irony. The problem stems not just from our difficulty in reconstructing the intended meaning, as we were able to do quite easily in a Jane Austen or George Eliot novel, nor even from our doubts about the intended meaning, as with the romantic ironist in his constantly veering position. Now we come rather to realise the impossibility of ever attaining any final meaning. Without a narrator on a reasonably secure pedestal, the truth becomes inaccessible; all that exists is flux, doubt, the unanswerable question. There is no place in the narrative economy for the reader except as a speculating decoder of the puzzles facing him. In this state of negativity, contradiction and paradox are forced upon us as the normal human condition. This unstable irony finds its ultimate expression in the literature of the absurd, in the novels of Beckett, for example, in their tragi-comic celebration of infinitely ironic existence.

★　　★　　★　　★　　★

Hazardous and murky though the area of irony may be, nevertheless, from the varying narrative stances of the ironist certain conclusions can be drawn about the nature and place of romantic irony.

In spite of its name, romantic irony is not primarily a historical phenomenon, as Ingrid Strohschneider-Kors maintains.[32] Though she does subsequently concede that it anticipates modern art,[33] she considers romantic irony as essentially a product of the Romantic movement. It was certainly the Romantics, notably Friedrich Schlegel and Solger, who recognised the importance of a particular kind of irony in art, and who attempted to formulate a theory of romantic irony. That theory is a direct outgrowth of the Romantics' *Welt-* and *Kunstanschauung*. But it is erroneous to tie the practice of romantic irony too closely to the emergence of the theory. As a distinctive narrative stance, the type of irony commonly known as 'romantic irony' clearly existed before Friedrich Schlegel's definition – witness *Tristram Shandy* and *Jacques le fataliste et son maître*, not to mention *Don Quixote*. The interpretation of romantic irony as a historical phenomenon is vitiated also by its continuance long after the end of the specific early nineteenth century literary movement. Its survival and development in twentieth century art is widely acknowledged: 'To study Romantic Irony is to discover how modern Romanticism could be, or, if you like, how Romantic Modernism is',[34] claims Muecke, who points to the novels of Thomas Mann as the best examples of romantic irony, and adduces this as evidence of 'Schlegel's astonishing ability to see in Romanticism the seeds of modernism'.[35] That is, perhaps, something of an overstatement; Schlegel can hardly be credited with explicit foresight of modernism, even though his theory did sow its seeds, and his vision was always directed to the future.

The conception of romantic irony as a historical phenomenon is, therefore, in need of some modification. The approach of the romantic ironist is an archetypal one, not necessarily limited to any historical period or periods. It does at certain times become more prevalent, and those times coincide with an increase of self-consciousness. There can be no doubt of the integral connection between romantic irony and the artist's consciousness of his role as a creative artist. The Romantic period, with its emphasis on individualism, subjectivity and the divine powers of the artist, was obviously one such age of elevated self-consciousness. Another is the early twentieth century, under the impact of Freud and the probing of consciousness in psycho-analysis. At both these historical moments, the intellectual climate was such as to breed the self-awareness that fosters romantic irony. Thus, romantic irony was prominent at the turn of the eighteenth to nineteenth centuries, and again in the early twentieth century. A historical pattern can evidently be traced of its outbreaks, so to speak, but this does not preclude its appearance at other times. The obvious parallel is to a disease that may long be present in isolated cases, and that may then, under special circumstances, become more prevalent. Similarly, romantic irony is both an archetypal and a historical phenomenon.

Equally complex is the relationship of romantic irony to other kinds of irony. It seems superfluous, particularly in the light of recent literary criticism, to reiterate that irony – romantic or otherwise – is much more than merely a rhetorical device. By its very nature, it always implies a certain critical detachment from the immediately present reality, and with this, a movement towards an alternative that is tacitly posited. In psychological terms, irony could be described as a form of perspectivism, the capacity to perceive several different possibilities concurrently. On the philosophical plane, irony may be seen as a process of relativisation, whereby the definity of the single simple affirmation is undermined by the more or less strongly articulated suggestion of other, perhaps conflicting, options. In the ironist's narrative stance, this process of relativisation is apparent. It is still at an embryonic stage with the impersonal ironist, who operates from the security of a moral centre and an external narrative position, and who lets us glimpse a carefully controlled image deviant from the ostensible surface. With the romantic ironist, that relativisation has made significant advances. His ambivalence towards both the world or reality and the work of his imagination marks a crucial turning-point in the use of irony. His narrative stance alongside his creation is part of his equivocal approach. His comments, his interruptions of the plot and of the illusion, his questions, are the concrete incarnations of his own doubts. No longer is there a self-assured narrator critical of things he rejects, as in the case of Jane Austen and George Eliot, whose irony springs as much from an affirmation of values they cherish as from a disparagement of those they censure. With the romantic ironist, this sureness has gone. In trying to penetrate the higher realms of the infinite, the Romantics often forfeited their solid foothold in a world of definities. What is more, by substituting aesthetic for moral criteria they laid themselves open to a degree of doubt that could be overwhelming. The manifestation of that pervading doubt comes in romantic irony, which denotes a check to the aspirations of romantic subjectivity, and which carries with it at least a hint of the failure of the romantic quest. Following the decisive impetus it received from romantic irony, the process of relativisation gained increasing momentum. With the third narrative stance, that of the ironist from within, the objective viewpoint has been obliterated. What remains is the subjective vision, and a half-hearted search for standards that can never be more than conjectural anyway. There is, obviously, a line of continuity from romantic irony to this 'new irony';[36] the self-consciousness, the doubting, the ambiguity and the paradoxicality, already inherent in romantic irony, become with the new irony dominant, engulfing, and corrosive.

Insofar as ambiguity, doubt and paradoxicality are traits of all irony, romantic irony is not severed from the main stream as a peculiarity wholly set apart. But romantic irony is distinctive in two ways: first, in its tendency to formulate theories about irony, to systematise itself self-consciously, so to speak; secondly and more importantly, in the prominence given to those ambiguities, doubts and paradoxes. With the impersonal ironist, they are limited in extent and firmly controlled in the artistic and moral centre that is the narrator. With the romantic ironist, and even more with the new ironist from within, it is the questioning, the shifting, the disorientation that are in the forefront. The quantitative change in the ambiguity cannot be dissociated from a qualitative change.

There is a final irony about romantic irony. It was conceived as a forceful assertion of the creative artist's freedom. For the Romantics the artist was a superior being, able not only to look with what Blake dismissed as 'My Corporeal or Vegetative Eye',[37] but also to perceive with the eye of the imagination the immanent ideal beyond the physical reality. He was designated as the 'seer', the 'voyant',[38] to use Rimbaud's later term. His irony was to be the expression of his superiority; it signifies his spiritual ability to fly – 'ein geistiges Fliegenkönnen',[39] is Ricarda Huch's vivid phrase. And irony was also to be the means of transcendence, the path of progression to the higher realm following the supposed annihilation of the finite.[40] That was the lofty intention of romantic irony. Its realisation was quite other, as we have seen, for it lead not to transcendence and progression, but to reduction and dishevelment. The movement it provoked was not in the ascendant, but a downward spiral. For romantic irony has 'etwas leicht Vexatorisches' ('something slightly vexatory'), 'die Möglichkeit eines Umschlags in die dunkle Kehrseite ihrer selbst'[41] ('the potential for an inversion into its own dark reverse side'). It was, in fact, this that predominated. In the discrepancy between its ideal aims and its concrete effects, romantic irony was a victim of its own processes.

NOTES TO CHAPTER 2

1. Johann Wolfgang von Goethe, *Werke*, ed. Erich Trunz (Munich: Beck, 1975) vol. xiii, p. 317.
2. D. C. Muecke, *The Compass of Irony* (London: Methuen, 1969) p. 181.
3. Raymond Immerwahr, 'The Subjectivity or Objectivity of Friedrich Schlegel's Poetic Irony', *Germanic Review*, xxvi (1951) 184.
4. Immerwahr, *Germanic Review*, xxvi, pp. 172–91.
5. Ernst Behler, *Klassische Ironie, Romantische Ironie, Tragische Ironie* (Darmstadt: Wissenschaftliche Buchgesellschaft, 1972) p. 148.
6. Muecke, *The Compass of Irony*, pp. 52–98.
7. Wayne C. Booth, *A Rhetoric of Irony* (Chicago: Chicago Univ. Press, 1974).
8. Muecke, *The Compass of Irony*, pp. 159–215.

9. Friedrich Schlegel, *Ideen*, No. 69, in *Kritische Ausgabe*, ed. Ernst Behler, Hans Eichner and Jean-Jacques Anstett (Paderborn: Schöningh) vol. ii (1967) p. 263.

10. See Ingrid Strohschneider-Kors, *Die romantische Ironie in Theorie und Gestaltung* (Tübingen: Niemeyer, 1960) pp. 59–63; Helmut Prang, *Die romantische Ironie* (Darmstadt: Wissenschaftliche Buchgesellschaft, 1972) pp. 8–15; Beda Allemann, *Ironie und Dichtung*, 2nd ed. (Pfullingen: Neske, 1969) pp. 55–82; Bernhard Heimrich, *Fiktion und Fiktionsironie in Theorie und Dichtung der deutschen Romantik* (Tübingen: Niemeyer, 1968) pp. 52–65; Raymond Immerwahr, *Germanic Review*, xxvi, 177–9; Ernst Behler, *Klassische Ironie, Romantische Ironie, Tragische Ironie*, pp. 67–73.

11. Booth, *A Rhetoric of Irony*, pp. 5–6.

12. Benjamin F. Bart, 'Art, Energy and Aesthetic Distance', in *'Madame Bovary' and the Critics*, ed. Benjamin F. Bart (New York: New York Univ. Press, 1966) pp. 73–105.

13. Bart, *'Madame Bovary' and the Critics*, p. 87

14. Wayne C. Booth, 'The Self-Conscious Narrator in Comic Fiction before *Tristram Shandy*', *Publications of the Modern Language Association of America*, lxvii (1952) 165.

15. Schlegel, *Ideen*, No. 69, in *Kritische Ausgabe*, vol. ii, p. 263.

16. Karl W. F. Solger, *Vorlesungen über Ästhetik*, ed. K. W. L. Heyse (Leipzig, 1829) p. 247.

17. Adam Müller, *Kritische, ästhetische und philosophische Schriften*, ed. Walter Schroeder and Werner Siebert (Berlin: Luchterhand, 1967) vol. i, p. 238.

18. Schlegel, *Athenäum*, No. 238, in *Kritische Ausgabe*, vol. ii, p. 204.

19. It is worth nothing in this context the see-saw balance between emotionality and irony in the different literatures during the Romantic period. Irony is most pronounced where there is least emphasis on feeling (i.e. in Germany), and conversely, least apparent where the expression of personal emotion is most to the fore (i.e. in France).

20. Strohschneider-Kors, *Die romatische Ironie*, p. 201 *et seq.*

21. Schlegel, *Athenäum*, No. 116, in *Kritische Ausgabe*, vol. ii, p. 183.

22. Schlegel, *Philosophische Lehrjahre*, in *Kritische Ausgabe*, vol. xviii, part ii (1962) p. 668.

23. Schlegel, *Athenäum*, No. 51, in *Kritische Ausgabe*, vol. ii, p. 172.

24. Muecke, *The Compass of Irony*, p. 165.

25. Muecke, *The Compass of Irony*, p. 164.

26. Heimrich, *Fiktion und Fiktionsironie*, pp. 127–8. Heimrich cites the term 'Indifferenzpunkt' from Brentano's *Vorerinnerung* to *Ponce de Leon*. The prompter sits at the 'point of indifference' while we have lost the perspective which enables us to decide whether it is the actor or the audience that is on stage.

27. Denis Diderot, *Jacques le fataliste et son maître* (Paris: Gallimard, 1973) pp. 83–4.

28. Booth, 'The Self-Conscious Narrator', p. 177.

29. Schlegel, *Lyceum*, No. 48, in *Kritische Ausgabe*, vol. ii, p. 153.

30. Schlegel, *Lyceum*, No. 42, in *Kritische Ausgabe*, vol. ii, p. 152.

31. '. . . die gesamte geschichtliche Wirklichkeit verneint, um Platz zu schaffen für eine selbstgeschaffene Wirklichkeit; nämlich die einer überspannten

Subjektivität.' S. A. Kierkegaard, *Gesammelte Werke*, ed. Emanuel Hirsch (Düsseldorf: Diederich, 1961) vol. xxxi, p. 280.

32. Strohschneider-Kors, *Die romatische Ironie*, p. 1.
33. Strohschneider-Kors, *Die romantische Ironie*, p. 434: 'das von der Romantik konzipierte Prinzip der künstlerischen Ironie und die mit dieser Konzeption hervorgehobene Möglichkeit der Kunst trägt eine gewisse Antizipation von Problemen der modernen Kunst in sich.'
34. Muecke, *The Compass of Irony*, p. 182.
35. Muecke, *The Compass of Irony*, p. 186.
36. See Benjamin de Mott, 'The New Irony,' *The American Scholar*, 31 (Winter 1961–62), 108–19.
37. William Blake, *Vision of the Last Judgement*, in *Complete Writings*, ed. Geoffrey Keynes (London: Oxford Univ. Press, 1966) p. 617.
38. Arthur Rimbaud, *Oeuvres complètes* (Paris: Gallimard, 1954) p. 270.
39. Ricarda Huch, *Die Blütezeit der Romantik* (Leipzig: Insel, 1901) p. 285.
40. See Strohschneider-Kors, *Die romantische Ironie*, p. 235 for an exposition of the three stages of romantic irony: '*Bewusstsein und Reflexion*', '*Annihilation*'; '*Aufhebung von Fixiertem und Bedingtem*'; and 'unaufhörliches Transzendieren, Progressivität'. Italics are author's.
41. Allemann, *Ironie und Dichtung*, p. 22.

3 The Romantic Hero, or is he an Anti-Hero?

The Romantic hero has become an archetypal figure in literature. His psyche has repeatedly been analysed, his geneaology traced, his persona categorised into various prototypes, and his relationship to society scrutinised. His pre-eminence in the writings of the Romantic period is such as to have provoked the contention that 'there was in the Romantic movement a distinctive heroic tradition',[1] indeed that 'the Romantic Age was our last great age of heroes'.[2] The emphasis in that phrase should, however, lie on the word 'last', for the Romantic hero, in spite of his dominant position, is already well on the way to the modern anti-hero. Perhaps that was in fact one of the sources of the fascination he evidently exercised: his essential ambiguity both reflected and appealed to a period of transition, that looked at one and the same time backwards and forwards.

In their preoccupation with heroism, the Romantics were heirs to the eighteenth century. The youthful rebels of the Storm and Stress in the 1770s worshipped human greatness in all its aspects: that of the creative genius, the thinker, the statesman, the religious leader, as well as the warrior's traditional heroism. It was also the attractiveness of its heroics that played a large part in the disproportionately fervid response to Ossian throughout Europe. With the advent of Napoleon, it almost seemed as if the Ossianic world of heroism were to become reality in early nineteenth century Europe.

But from the outset there were signs of a certain unease with the heroic ideal. The protagonists of the Storm and Stress, such as Goethe's Götz von Berlichingen and Schiller's Karl Moor, are already at some remove from the customary norms of prescriptive heroism in their moral equivocalness. Nor, for that matter, does the behaviour of the Ossianic warrior really correspond to

40

conventional concepts of heroism, comprising, as it does, more savagery than chivalry. As for the living model of the hero, Napoleon, he soon proved a bitter disappointment to many, including Goethe and Beethoven, who changed the dedication of his Eroica Symphony when Napoleon had himself proclaimed Emperor. The substitue phrase, 'to the memory of a great man' strongly suggests the demise of the hero in the opening years of the nineteenth century. Napoleon's ignominious end in exile, in glaring antithesis to his glorious rise, seemed to confirm the hollowness of heroism in the modern world. The profound shock of disillusionment that shattered European youth on the collapse of Napoleon is vividly evoked by Musset in the second chapter of *La Confession d'un enfant du siècle*:

> Les enfants regardaient tout cela, pensant toujours que l'ombre de César allait débarquer à Cannes et souffler sur ces larves; mais le silence continuait toujours, et l'on ne voyait flotter dans le ciel que la pâleur des lis. Quand les enfants parlaient de gloire, on leur disait: 'Faites-vous prêtres'; quand ils parlaient d'ambition: 'Faites-vous prêtres'; d'espérance, d'amour, de force, de vie: 'Faites-vous prêtres'![3]

> (The children watched all this, thinking day after day that Caesar's ghost would land at Cannes and breathe life into these spectres; but the silence continued day after day, and only the pale lilies swayed in the sky. When the children spoke of glory, they were told: 'Become priests'; when they spoke of ambition, 'Become priests'; of hope, of love, of strength, of life: 'Become priests'!)

It is from among these thwarted 'gladiateurs', aware only of their 'misère insupportable',[4] that the anti-hero was to emerge.

Thus the Romantics, while apparently in search of the paradigmatic hero, no longer wholly believed in his pristine existence, even if they were not yet ready to admit this openly. Byron's famous invocation for *Don Juan*, 'I want a hero' is, as Harry Levin has so astutely pointed out, 'just as significant of its time as were the respective invocations of the *Aeneid* and the *Orlando Furioso* for theirs. It is the cry of a century which is often considered a century of hero-worship, the quest of an age forever seeking and never quite finding what Lermontov styled *A Hero of*

Our Time.'[5] But that title, *A Hero of Our Time*, is conceded by the narrator of Lermontov's novel to be 'a wicked irony'[6] in that Pechorin is no more heroic than Don Juan. The embarrassment vis-à-vis the new style pseudo-hero is fully voiced by Foscolo when his Jacopo Ortis writes: 'Non so mai di che nome voi altri saggi chiamate chi troppo presto ubbidisce al proprio cuore; perchè di certo non è un eroe; ma è forse vile per questo?'[7] ('I never know what you sophisticates call the man who too promptly obeys the dictates of his heart; for he certainly is not a hero; but is he any the less for that?') The predicament of Foscolo and his European contemporaries is clearer than its solution. For if the term 'hero' is no longer entirely appropriate to the characters portrayed by the Romantics, nor is 'anti-hero' in its modern connotation, which I take to have originated in Dostoyevsky's *Notes from Underground*.[8] Even though the Romantic period still wanted a grandiose hero, what it actually produced was a hybrid half-way between the hero and the anti-hero.

In some ways the Romantic hero does still fulfil the traditional heroic role. First, his attractive appearance often makes him a sort of *homme fatal*. Almost invariably he is a gentleman, a member of the leisured class at ease financially. Both his handsomeness and his freedom from mundane concerns raise him to the level of an idealised, glamorous figure sharply distinguished from the characteristic modern anti-hero with his petty subsistence-level anxieties, his frequent physical imperfections, his embroilment in the grotesque messiness of daily living. All this is alien to the Romantic hero who exists, as in Caspar David Friedrich's painting, *Mountaineer in a Misty Landscape*, on a lofty mountain-top high above everyday reality.

He is the hero also in the technical sense as the chief protagonist in a work, and here again Friedrich's picture is illuminating. Looming at its very middle as the sole human figure, the mountaineer demonstrates visually the Romantic hero's dominant presence. It is no coincidence that so many works of this period bear as their title simply the name of the main character: *René*, *Obermann*, *Hernani*, *Ruy Blas*, *Chatterton*, *Lorenzaccio*, *Antony*, *Eugene Onegin*, *Don Juan*, *Manfred*, *Cain*, *Werner*, *Marino Faliero*, *Lara*, *Peter Schlemihl* etc. Even where the original title was more complex e.g. *Die Leiden des jungen Werthers*, *Le ultime lettere di Jacopo Ortis*, *Childe Harold's Pilgrimage*, instinctively custom has abbreviated it to the essential name. In this particular context the Romantic hero is, in fact, more literally the 'hero' than most of his predecessors had been. He holds the centre of works whose primary purpose is the presentation of his character. He over-shadows others almost to the point of exclusion; the focus is concentrated on him, at the expense of the other personae, who often act merely as a foil or a sounding-board for the hero. In many instances their chief function is that of recipient of his letters or confidences (e.g. Wilhelm in *Werther*, Lorenzo in *Jacopo Ortis*, the Père Souël in *René*). Even the women who are the object of his passion are scantily sketched, while his opponents in drama, though more fully bodied forth than the surrounding figures in the narrative, still remain insignificant relative to the 'hero'. All are attendant on him, dwarfed by his towering stature, that seems virtually to blot out all else. It is with some surprise that one realises how minimal is our perception of the subsidiary figures, such as Albert in *Werther*, Odoardo in *Jacopo Ortis*, Maxim Maximich in *A Hero of Our Time*, John Bell in *Chatterton*, Roth in *Der Waldbruder*, Lensky in *Eugene Onegin*, Smith in *La Confession d'un enfant du siècle*, Don Salluste in *Ruy Blas*. The Romantic hero is certainly the 'hero' in this respect.

But even this 'heroism' has a sinister side. For the Romantic hero's dominance stems not from his activity, but from the interest in his psyche, since his heroic assertion is the egocentric one of his own personality, far indeed from the hero's traditional commitment to a cause outside himself. This reversal is an outcome of the Romantic cult of the exceptional individual, who could be exceptional in a negative as well as a positive direction, bearing traces of the Gothic villain in his mentality, and the mark of Cain on his fateful physiognomy. The departure from the earlier concept of heroism was further encouraged by the re-placement of the old ethos of duty by the new ethos of feeling, with its implicit trust in the instincts and impulses of the heart.[9] Thus even though the Romantic hero is undeniably the 'hero' of the works in which he appears, his 'heroism' is of a particular kind. For his overwhelming presence is the expression of that total self-absorption that makes his universe – and that of the work in which he appears – pivot entirely on his idiosyncratic ego. In such egocentric self-assertion lies one of the crucial distinctions between the archetypal hero and the anti-hero.

The transformation of hero into anti-hero is a process of reduction. It was activated during the Romantic period by the protagoists' *Ichschmerz* (ego-suffering). That term, coined by William Rose,[10] offers a more apt description of the Romantic hero's state of mind than the more usual *Weltschmerz* or *mal du siècle*. For the roots of his affliction lie neither in his grief for the world, as *Weltschmerz* would seem to imply, nor in conditions specific to his time, although these contribute to his discontent. The ultimate source of his malady resides in that solipsistic self-absorption that entraps him in a vicious circle. The proud awareness of himself as an exceptional being leads to a cultivation of his differentness and to an incessant brooding on his state. Eventually he reaches a depth of self-involution where his introverted sense of self completely distorts his perception of outer reality so that he sinks even further into himself. This attitude represents the antithesis to that of the archetypal hero. The latter's essentially outward-looking orientation, his role as a leader of men, his readiness to sacrifice himself to the cause he has espoused: all these traditionally heroic features are in diametric contrast to the *Ichschmerz* that is the core of the Romantic hero.

This *Ichschmerz* determines his relationship to others as well as to himself. Whereas the hero is often envisaged as a saviour, a redeemer, intent on the common weal, the Romantic hero all too frequently exerts a disruptive, indeed destructive force. 'I loved her, and destroy'd her!': Manfred's confession could come from the lips of many a Romantic hero: 'Not with my hand, but heart, which broke her heart;/It gazed on mine, and wither'd'.[11] What a litter of broken hearts and broken lives the Romantic hero leaves in his wake: Faust's seduction of Gretchen, Werther's intrusion into the marriage of Lotte and Albert, René's fatal attachment to his sister, Jacopo Ortis's disturbance of Teresa's life, Octave's cruelty to Brigitte, Pechorin's teasing of Mary and his neglect of Bella, Chatterton's undoing of Kitty Bell, Antony's murder of Adèle (albeit allegedly for her own good!). In each case it is ultimately the Romantic hero's egocentric pursuit of self-satisfaction that is the cause of the misfortune he spreads. And only rarely is he even conscious of his guilt, as is Manfred; generally his self-centredness is such as to blind him to the havoc he is causing in an innocent indifference that verges on the diabolical.

His absorption in his own inner problems also undermines the force of his much vaunted rebellion, for his primary confrontation is with himself rather than with society.[12] Though he is irked by a society whose artificial values he rejects with vehemence, he makes little or no positive attempt at reform. His antagonism to society takes the negative form of a withdrawal: in many instances it is a literal retreat into the remote backwoods, after the manner of Rousseau's 'promeneur solitaire'. Werther, Obermann, and Herz (in Lenz's *Der Waldbruder*) have fled from urban life into quiet villages, René is with the noble savages of Louisiana, Jacopo Ortis in the Euganean Hills. Far from combating the social ills of his day, as the hero of the Storm and Stress had still endeavoured to do, the Romantic hero chooses instead the path of evasion. If he considers himself 'a glorious antagonist of society', it is, as Victor Brombert has pointed out, 'often with duplicity'. For 'typically, the Romantic hero is obsessed with the difficulty of defining borders between the self and the non-self. Typically also, he is self-conscious, paralyzed by doubt, and essentially in rebellion against his own background.'[13] Thus his rebellion too is fixated on his own position; and its practical effect is, paradoxically, to intensify his *Ichschmerz* since the solitary wanderer in the woods is free to fill his days with 'rêveries'.

But indulgence in his reveries serves only to plunge him more and more deeply into solipsistic gloom. So the Romantic hero becomes not only destructive to those around him, but also self-destructive. In this he is already close to the anti-hero. In contrast, however, to his twentieth-century counterpart, who accepts the hopelessness of his life with an ironic smile for the very reason that he stands beyond hope, the Romantic hero, at least at the outset, still tends to cherish certain dreams. He believes that salvation may come from communion with the beauties of nature, from the true love of a fine woman, from commitment to art. His story follows initially the pattern of a quest, in which he may reach moments of euphoria when he thinks himself nigh to fulfilment. But all too soon comes that disillusionment that is an integral part of the process of reduction from hero to anti-hero. The Romantic hero has to face not just the thwarting of one particular wish: that nature can be cruelly unsympathetic, the woman of his desires beyond reach, and society unreceptive to art. The experience is climacteric in his life, making him aware of the intrinsic futility of all willing and seeking. This signifies the failure of his deeper quest for the meaning of existence, a failure of self-realisation, a drastic loss of hope and of faith in himself as well as in the world. Obermann's summary of this experience is exemplary in its brevity: 'L'illusion a duré près d'un mois dans sa force; un seul incident l'a dissipée. C'est alors que toute l'amertume d'une vie décolorée et fugitive vint remplir mon âme'[14] ('The full force of the illusion held for nearly a month; a single incident dispelled it. It was then that the bitterness of a pallid, rootless existence took possession of my soul'). It is that single incident of crucial reversal, in various guises, that forms the pivot of the Romantic hero's tale. His apparently disproportionate response to a specific disappointment is comprehensible in the light of the ontological and psychological background. It is not, for instance, merely Lotte's and Kitty's inaccessibility that drive Werther and Chatterton to suicide; these episodes act as a catalyst to the Romantic hero's stark confrontation with the fundamental hopelessness of his life.

Underlying the Romantic hero's final despair is the perception of the 'abîme ouvert à mes côtes'[15] ('the abyss gaping beside me') to cite René's appropriate image. 'Je trouve partout le vide'[16] ('I find everywhere emptiness'), Obermann exclaims, while Octave uses the same key-word in his comment: 'Il semble que l'homme soit vide, et qu'à force de descendre en lui il arrive à la dernière marche d'une spirale'[17] ('Man seems to be empty, and as he delves into himself he comes down to the last rung of a spiral'). Jacopo Ortis too reaches this point: 'ora anche l'illusione mi abbandona: – medito sul passato; m'affisso su i di che verranno; e non veggo che nulla'[18] ('now my illusions too are spent: – I think of the past; I contemplate the days to come; and I see only nothingness'). In less lofty but equally cogent manner, Lorenzo confides to the startled Philippe: 'Je me suis réveillé de mes rêves, rien de plus . . . Je connais la vie, et c'est une vilaine cuisine'[19] ('I have awoken from my dreams, that's all. . . . I know life, and it's a vile brew'), words that recall Byron's even more forthright dismissal of the 'nothingness of life' as 'not worth a potato'![20] The tone may run the whole gamut from such flippant scoffing to Faust's outbursts of angry despair, or the agonised anguish of Werther's final call to the God who has left him (diary entry 15 November) and his poignant question: 'was soll mir das?' ('what avails me all this?') in his diary entry of 30 November. Though the form may vary, the ultimate import is the same: the recognition of nil, *le néant*, that cast its shadow over the nineteenth century already and darkens the twentieth. At the nadir of the Romantic hero's life comes that point of utter negativity that represents the inversion of the Romantic quest, the bankruptcy of idealism.

Nowhere is this as evident as in that strange product of German Romanticism that appeared anonymously in 1804 under the title *Die Nachtwachen des Bonaventura (The Night Watches of Bonaventura)*. Its hero – though 'anti-hero' is wholly appropriate here – is a former poet who has become a nightwatchman. His name, Kreuzgang, with its multivalent associations to 'cross' and 'crossways', is indicative of his profound ambiguity. It is this Kreuzgang who, in a mixture of madness and sleep, experiences the horror of the ultimate dissolution of the self into nothingness:

Es stürmte wild um das Tollhaus her – ich lag am Gitter und schaute in die Nacht, ausser der am Himmel und auf Erden nichts weiter zu sehen war. Es war mir, als stände ich dicht am Nichts und riefe hinein, aber es gäbe keinen Ton mehr – ich erschrak, denn ich glaubte wirklich gerufen zu haben, aber ich hörte mich nur in mir ... Es dünkte mich, als entschlief ich. Da sah ich mich selbst mit mir allein im Nichts, nur in der weiten Ferne verglimmte noch die letzte Erde, wie ein auslöschender Funken – aber es war nur ein Gedanke von mir, der eben endete. Ein einziger Ton bebte schwer und ernst durch die Öde – es war die ausschlagende Zeit, und die Ewigkeit trat jetzt ein. Ich hatte jetzt aufgehört, alles andere zu denken, und dachte nur mich selbst! Kein Gegenstand war ringsum aufzufinden als das grosse schreckliche Ich, das an sich selbst zehrte und im Verschlingen stets sich selbst wiedergebar. Ich sank nicht, denn es war kein Raum mehr, ebenso wenig schien ich emporzuschweben. Die Abwechslung war zugleich mit der Zeit verschwunden, und es herrschte eine fürchterliche ewig öde Langeweile. Ausser mir, versuchte ich mich zu vernichten – aber ich blieb und fühlte mich unsterblich![21]

(A storm was raging wildly around the madhouse – I lay against the bars and looked into the night beyond which nothing was to be seen in heaven or on earth. I felt as though I were standing on the verge of Nothing and called into it, but there was no more sound – I took fright, for I believed that I had really called, but I heard only myself within myself ... It seemed to me that I fell asleep. Then I saw myself all alone in nothingness, only in the remote distance the last ray of earth was fading away like a dying spark – but it was only a thought of mine, just ending. A single tone quavered solemnly and ominously through the desolation – it was time expiring, and now eternity set in. I had ceased now to think of all else, and thought only myself! No object was to be found all around other than the great terrible I, that was consuming itself and in the devouring was constantly regenerating itself. I did not sink, for there was no more space, nor did I seem to float upwards. Change had disappeared together with time, and a terrible, eternal, desolate tedium reigned. Beside myself, I tried to destroy myself – but I remained and knew myself to be indestructible!)

This description of the ego devouring itself to end in nothingness is a most vivid and appropriate image for the confrontation with the void. Here, in its full force, we encounter what Korff[22] has aptly characterised as 'negative Romanticism': a destruction of the world, a reduction to nothingness that is the final implacable consequence of that boundless self-idolatry that marks the Romantic hero, and, incidentally, turns him into an anti-hero. When man arrogates to himself the role of divinity, God is removed from the universe. That this is already implicit in the writing of the Romantic period has been well documented by Karl S. Guthke in *Die Mythologie der entgötterten Welt* (Gottingen: Vandenhoeck and Ruprecht, 1971). By a final ironic twist *Ichschmerz* indeed becomes *Weltschmerz* in its original sense – sorrow over the world – when that world is eaten away by the corrosive acid of egocentricity. This situation, so familiar to Huysmans' Des Esseintes (in *A Rebours*) and to his fellow *fin de siècle* aesthetes as well as to the anti-heroes of our own century, was by no means unknown to the Romantics. The path from *Ichschmerz* to nihilism, the archetypal path of the anti-hero, is already trodden by the Romantic hero.

This insidious process of dissolution is reflected in the artistic form too. In this respect also the works of the Romantic period adumbrate the mutation from heroic to anti-heroic shape. Many of the changes in the late eighteenth and early nineteenth centuries devolve from the centrality of the solipsistic hero. First, as has already been noted, his prominence is at the expense of other characters, who are more often than not sketched only scantily and in relation to him. Secondly, it results in a marked preponderance of self-analysis; in drama the action is slowed by lengthy self-revelatory monologues by the chief protagonist. Taken to extremes, this leads to a weakening of the dramatic tension in a series of lyrical scenes that are a vehicle for the exhibition of a psyche, as in Byron's *Manfred*, for example. In the novel there is an extraordinary growth in the first person narrative. Either the 'hero' confesses his life (e.g. *René, La Confession d'un enfant du siècle*), or he records it in letters and diaries (e.g. *Werther, Jacopo Ortis, Obermann*). But whereas the eighteenth-century *roman épistolaire* had presented the correspondence of a number of people (e.g. *Clarissa Harlowe, Les Liaisons dangereuses, La Nouvelle Héloïse*), often cleverly exploiting the possibilities of the multiple threads for the structure of the plot, the Romantic novel in letters almost invariably is limited to the writing of a single person with, at most, a few interpolated notes, such as those of Lotte in *Werther*, and the closing comments of a friend-narrator (e.g. Wilhelm in *Werther*, Lorenzo in *Jacopo Ortis*) to bury the deceased letter-writer. The viewpoint is thus largely restricted to a single perspective, which makes it as difficult for the reader as for the 'hero' to assess the realities of the situation with any kind of objectivity. It is only by surmise from the odd interspersed phrase that we can try to redress the balance and see the protagonist and his problems from the outside. But perhaps it is mistaken for the reader to make any such effort, for these novels are, as George Sand so well put it, '*monodies* mystérieuses et sévères où toutes les grandeurs et les misères humaines se confessent et se dévoilent'[23] ('mysterious and austere *monodies* in which human greatness and human misery are confessed and revealed'). The reader is invited to suspend his critical reasoning and to yield, along with the protagonist, to the enveloping mood.

This blurring of the contours is equally evident in the conduct of the action, for the Romantic hero's course often foreshadows the drifting of the modern anti-hero. 'Dangling', to borrow Saul Bellow's striking term from his early novel, *Dangling Man*, is virtually the antithesis of the heroic ideal with its purposeful conquest, its resolute protagonist, prompt in decision, courageous in deed, and above all, active in the pursuit of his aims even unto death. The heroic saga in literature focuses on the hero's adventures, his grappling with the momentous 'test' in one form or another, to a triumphant resolution. Reflecting the hero's characteristically ascendant curve, the action moves forward in a linear progression. The contrast with the Romantic anti-hero is marked. His typical reaction is not confrontation of the problem, but rather a continued evasiveness. His antagonism to the values of society leads him to no energetic opposition, only to withdrawal to a realm of his own, where he may cultivate the Utopia of his pipe-dreams. When this – predictably – fails to satisfy him, he tends to seek salvation in other climes. It is arguable that the Romantic hero's often-noted restlessness is the outer expression of an existence patterned to flight: flight from the world, and at the same time from himself. So he drifts, hesitates, prevaricates, all the while slowly retreating from any demands made on him. He does not act until he is driven into an inescapable impasse, and then often his actions are self-destructive. Yet, significantly, the prospect of death at his own hand induces a state akin to euphoria: at long last a decision releases him from the paralysis of his passivity. One of the consequences of this emphasis on inner dilemmas, on the exploration of character is an attrition of outer action. *Obermann*, for instance, records a series of states of consciousness; *A Hero of Our Time* is a fragmentary string of episodes, while *Eugene Onegin*, *Der Waldbruder*, *La Confession d'un enfant du siècle* leave the central character unhappily embroiled in an unresolved situation. The only logical end for the Romantic hero is death, as in *Werther*, *Jacopo Ortis*, *René*, *Chatterton*, *Lorenzaccio*, *Antony*. His physical annihilation is the natural conclusion to the downward slope of his life. For his curve, contrary to that of the traditional hero, is a declining one; his life literally falls away into that nothingness that faces him, just as action peters out into the lyricism of the monody.

In this devolution from hero to anti-hero one further element plays a decisive role, namely irony, and more specifically self-irony. Irony, as Lionel Trilling has succinctly defined it, is the capacity 'to establish a disconnection between the speaker and his interlocutor, or between the speaker and that which is being spoken about, or even between the speaker and himself'.[24] It is particularly in this last sense of a disconnection between the speaker and himself that irony is one of the crucial tests of the anti-hero. His alienation has progressed so far as to breed a genuine detachment not only from his world, but also from himself. Often, his self-mockery has a bitter flavour; nonetheless its very presence denotes a capacity to stand back from his own problems and, to some extent at least, to rise above them by viewing them from a point outside himself. Because of this dual vision the anti-hero is frequently a tragi-comic figure; with characteristic ambivalence he sees the black humour as well as the pathos of his situation. He may in fact be the clown masking behind grotesque laughter his shattering glimpse of the abyss.

This most advanced stage of anti-heroism remains by and large foreign to the Romantic hero. He is still too full of the certainty of himself to engage in a fundamental questioning of his own persona. The Romantics could, and did, venture a radical reassessment of accepted assumptions, but that revaluation was always undertaken from the relative *terra firma* of a wholehearted belief in the validity of the subjective perception. The infallibility of the ego was the foundation-stone of Fichte's *Wissenschaftslehre*, that manual of Romantic subjectivism, which posited the absolute validity of the ego almost as a categorical imperative. Against this background, the Romantic hero was not yet prepared for the elemental self-doubt implicit in any deeper irony.

Nevertheless, traces of irony are apparent at various levels and in varying degree. A critical attitude towards the hero begins to emerge, for instance, from some of the comments of those around him, though this strain is of necessity muted in the first person narrative. But Lotte's verdict: 'Werther, Sie sind sehr krank'[25] ('Werther, you are very ill') implies a marked reduction in his standing. The final criticism of Old Souël, in Chateaubriand's *René*, is even more pointed as he asks this 'jeune présomptueux' ('presumptuous young man'): 'Que faites-vous seul au fond des forêts où vous consumez vos jours, négligeant tous vos devoirs?'[26] ('What are you doing all alone consuming your days in the depths of the forests and neglecting your duties?') These gentle, friendly reproaches soon acquire a sharper sting and a more prominent place. Both *Der Waldbruder* and *La Confession d'un enfant du siècle*, a relatively late product of Romanticism, leave no doubt as to the negative judgement on the hero.

On a different plane, the Romantic hero is subjected to direct or oblique critical questioning on the part of the author. The obvious example is Byron, whose constant sardonic commen-

tary on his titular hero's adventures in *Don Juan* effectively pricks
the heroic bubble and cuts his character to size.

> In thoughts like these true wisdom may discern
>   Longings sublime, and aspirations high,
> Which some are born with, but the most part learn
>   To plague themselves withal, they know not why:
> 'Twas strange that one so young should thus concern
>   His brain about the action of the sky;
> If *you* think 'twas philosophy that this did,
> I can't help thinking puberty assisted.
>
> He pored upon the leaves, and on the flowers,
>   And heard a voice in all the winds; and then
> He thought of wood-nymphs and immortal bowers,
>   And how the goddesses came down to men:
> He miss'd the pathway, he forgot the hours,
>   And when he look'd upon his watch again,
> He found how much old Time had been a winner –
> He also found that he had lost his dinner.[27]

Like Byron, Pushkin disparages his own creature in his reiterated
barbs at Eugene Onegin. Lermontov, too, shows his ironic
attitude in the title he chooses for his story, *A Hero of Our Time*.
The Romantic hero was evidently not intended as an ideal;
Goethe conceived Werther as a warning, as did Chateaubriand
his René. Often the character's name in itself may be revealing,
or suggestive of an implicit irony: Lenz's protagonist in *Der
Waldbruder* is called Herz (heart), i.e. he is all sensibility (and little
sense); Sénancour's Obermann is a strange 'Superman' indeed;
how 'Worthy' is Werther? and to what is Chateaubriand's René
'Re-born'? At times the Romantic hero may evoke pity, but
frequently he is the butt of a ridiculing irony. He verges on a
tragi-comic figure of fun, already redolent of the modern anti-
hero.

But the Romantic hero lacks the modern anti-hero's ironic
self-detachment. It is not just that he takes himself so seriously;
his very idealism establishes absolute standards and lofty expectations which militate against the ironist's flexible relativism.
The source of his difficulty is perhaps an excess of sincerity.

'Werther', as Lionel Trilling has pointed out, 'is incapable of embodying this desperate comic wit; irony is beyond his comprehension. He is in all things the sincere man; even in his disintegration he struggles to be true to the self he must believe is his own.'[28] He was not able to achieve detachment from himself because 'his alienation did not proceed far enough'. This illuminating insight very neatly places the Romantic hero as a man of incipient alienation who has, however, not yet reached the full detachment of self-irony.

So the Romantic hero stands unhappily betwixt and between. Far indeed from the firm commitment of the traditional hero, he has not yet arrived at the anti-hero's blasé alienation. He dissociates himself from his world, to which he bears a tense, highly critical relationship, but his profound self-absorption precludes any genuine self-detachment. His questioning goes only to a certain point, where he evasively dismisses 'Qui sait? qui sait?' ('who knows?') as a 'parole infâme'[29] ('infamous phrase'). Unable or unwilling to confront the ultimate issues, the Romantic hero suddenly finds himself face to face with nothingness. He cannot take the great leap which would allow him to negotiate the abyss with a bitter laugh. Lacking ironic self-detachment and, hence, the ability to rise above his ills and those of the world with the tragi-comic shrug of the clown, he can but weep and go under. The modern anti-hero's defence mechanism is still beyond the Romantic hero's emotional range. Only Kreuzgang in *Die Nachtwachen des Bonaventura* has gone further. He is the burnt-out Romantic hero, the erstwhile poet who has become a night-watchman and, not by coincidence, in the process, 'ein Humorist' ('a humorist'), 'ein rein Toller'[30] ('a sheer madman'). He has discarded his own self to 'retire' into the guise of a nightwatchman, a detached ironical spectator. He represents, in all his incongruities, the closest approach during the Romantic period to an archetypal anti-hero.

In many respects, therefore, the Romantic hero already foreshadows the anti-hero: in his extreme self-consciousness, in his disillusioned questioning, in his confrontation of nothingness, in his destructiveness and self-destructiveness, in his tendency to query values, and through his presence to modulate literary forms. What he lacks as yet is the self-irony that is one of the crucial hallmarks of the true anti-hero. But the Romantic hero reflects an age whose questing and questioning was to undermine its own idealism, and to lead towards that ambivalence that is the ideological basis for the anti-hero. Unwittingly perhaps the Romantics initiated the move along this reductive path; and so, appropriately, their hero prefigures the anti-hero.

NOTES TO CHAPTER 3

1. Peter L. Thorslev, Jr., *The Byronic Hero. Types and Prototypes* (Minneapolis: Univ. of Minnesota Press, 1962) p. 185.
2. Thorslev, *The Byronic Hero*, p. 16.
3. Alfred de Musset, *Oeuvres complètes* (Paris: Garnier, n.d.) vol. vii, p. 6.
4. Musset, *Oeuvres complètes*, vol. vii, p. 11.
5. Harry T. Levin, 'Society as Its Own Historian', in *Contexts of Criticism* (Cambridge, Mass.: Harvard Univ. Press, 1957) p. 176.
6. Mikhail Lermontov, *A Hero of Our Time*, translated by Philip Longworth (London: The New English Library, 1962) p. 50.
7. Ugo Foscolo, *Le ultime lettere di Jacopo Ortis* (Milan: EFA, 1945) p. 33; letter of 22 November 1797.
8. Fyodor Dostoyevsky, *Notes from Underground*, Part Two, section X.
9. See Louis I. Bredvold, *The Natural History of Sensibility* (Detroit: Wayne State Univ. Press, 1962).
10. William Rose, *From Goethe to Byron: the Development of 'Weltschmerz' in German literature* (London: Routledge, 1924). The title is somewhat misleading because Rose deals primarily with the *Göttinger Dichterbund*, i.e. poets antecedent to Goethe.
11. George Gordon Byron, *Manfred*, scene ii, line 117ff.
12. See Frederick Garber, 'Self, Society, Value, and the Romantic Hero', *Comparative Literature*, xix, No. 4 (Fall 1967) 321 –33.
13. Victor Brombert, 'The Idea of the Hero', in *The Hero in Literature*, ed. Victor H. Brombert (New York: Fawcett, 1969) p. 19.
14. Etienne de Sénancour, *Obermann* (Paris: Charpentier, n.d.) p. 45.
15. François-René de Chateaubriand, *René* (New York: Oxford Univ. Press, 1926) p. 112.
16. Sénancour, *Obermann*, p. 24.
17. Musset, *Oeuvres complètes*, vol. vii, p. 300.
18. Foscolo, *Jacopo Ortis*, p. 162.
19. Musset, *Lorenzaccio*, act III, scene iii, line 327.
20. Byron, *Don Juan*, canto VII, stanzas iv and vi.
21. *Die Nachtwachen des Bonaventura* (Edinburgh Univ. Press, 1972) pp. 212–14.
22. H. A. Korff, *Geist der Goethezeit* (Leipzig: Koehler & Amelang, 1940) vol. iii, pp. 204–18.
23. Preface to Sénancour, *Obermann*, p. 1.
24. Lionel Trilling, *Sincerity and Authenticity* (Cambridge, Mass.: Harvard Univ. Press, 1971) p. 120.

25. Johann Wolfgang von Goethe, *Werke* (Salzburg: Bergland Verlag, 1949) vol. i, p. 449.
26. Chateaubriand, *René*, p. 141.
27. Byron, *Don Juan*, Canto I, stanzas xciii and xciv.
28. Trilling, *Sincerity and Authenticity*, p. 52.
29. Musset, *Oeuvres complètes*, vol. vii, p. 292.
30. *Die Nachtwachen des Bonaventura*, p. 38.

4 Mme de Staël's
De L'Allemagne:
a Misleading Intermediary

De L'Allemagne has long been established as one of the major intermediaries between France and Germany, a pillar of Franco-German literary relations. Goethe already recognised it 'als ein mächtiges Rüstzeug . . . , das in die chinesische Mauer antiqui-erter Vorurteile, die uns von Frankreich trennte, sogleich eine breite Lücke durchbrach, so dass man über den Rhein und, in Gefolge dessen, über den Kanal endlich von uns nähere Kenntnis nahm'[1] ('as a mighty weapon . . . , which immediately made a wide breach in the Chinese wall of antiquated prejudices that separated us from France, so that across the Rhine and thence across the Channel Germany at last came to be better known'). Subsequently *De L'Allemagne* became 'un guide littéraire',[2] often nicknamed the Bible of the Romantics, while Mme de Staël herself has been called 'essentiellement une inspiratrice du romantisme',[3] 'une prophétesse',[4] 'that fascinating old queen of Romanticism',[5] 'institutrice de toute une génération'[6] ('teacher to a whole generation'), and 'Mistress to an Age'.[7] There would seem to be some truth in the witticism attributed to the Duc de Berry, that there were at that time three great powers in Europe: England, Russia, and Mme de Staël.

The intrinsic importance of *De L'Allemagne* resides not so much in either the quality or the quantity of its reportage on German literature as in the fundamental changes of attitude which it implied and induced. These pertain to the relationship of the French to their own literary heritage as well as to their evaluation of the Germans as a cultural force. In both these areas *De L'Allemagne* marks a crucial turning-point. In the history of French poetry, as Margaret Gilman has pointed out in *The Idea of*

Poetry in France (Cambridge, Mass.: Harvard Univ. Press, 1958, p. 120) 'with Mme de Staël and *De L'Allemagne* the idea of a poetry different from that of the "great tradition" comes to the fore'. Gilman defines it further as 'a poetry fraught with emotion, enthusiasm, and imagery, possessed of a mysterious, even mystical quality' (p. 121). The kind of writing which *De L'Allemagne* revealed to the French was certainly very far from the Neoclassical manner to which they were accustomed. Therein lay one of the sources of its attraction to an age uneasily aware of the need to reform a pattern that was degenerating into a stale stereotype. In helping to provide a stimulus for a creative renewal of French poetry by showing fresh paths and possibilities, *De L'Allemagne* is of far-reaching significance. Moreover, its suggestion of Germany as a model for France was in itself a revolutionary reversal of the trend dominant until then. Throughout the seventeenth and eighteenth centuries Germany had looked to France for a cultural lead, its small courts admiring and aping Versailles. The French, on the other hand, barely disguised their contempt for their barbarian neighbour, whose literature they largely ignored, with the exception of a few idylls. Attempts had been made to improve and redress the current image of Germany as a boorish backwater; for instance, by Elie Fréron and Michael Huber in Paris in the mid-eighteenth century, and in the accounts of such travellers as Catteau-Calleville, Charles Villers and Benjamin Constant. But their earnest efforts to disseminate information had relatively little effect. It was not until Mme de Staël's demonstrative applause that a real change of attitude toward Germany occurred. Suddenly and startlingly, the despised laggard was held up not only as a daring innovator, but even as a potential teacher. In this respect, too, the importance of *De L'Allemagne* in the history of Franco-German literary relations can hardly be overestimated: quite simply, it denotes the beginning of a new epoch.

It is indeed its prominent position as one of the cornerstones of the nineteenth century that prompts and justifies this further analysis of its role as an intermediary. Partly because of the novelty of its content and partly because of the sensational circumstances of its publication in England following the ban by Napoleonic censure, *De L'Allemagne* made a tremendous impact. Six complete French editions appeared between 1814 and 1819 besides sundry extracts, reviews and five critical studies, and the years 1820 to 1870 witnessed fifteen further reprints. For long *De L'Allemagne* reigned supreme as the standard source of knowledge about German literature, not only in France, but also in England and the United States, where Mme de Staël's image of Germany was propagated by Carlyle and Ticknor respectively. This prompt acceptance, wide diffusion and lasting effect of the notions expounded in *De L'Allemagne* makes it all the more imperative that we should attain clarity about its nature and efficacy as an intermediary. And it is no diminution of Mme de Staël's total achievement to point out some of the misconceptions she harboured and their curious consequences.

★   ★   ★   ★   ★

De L'Allemagne is generally reputed to contain an account of German Romanticism which inspired the nascent French Romantic movement. The latter part of that proposition, viz. that *De L'Allemagne* inspired the French Romantics, is certainly true, but not, as is frequently supposed, by its revelation of German Romanticism. Herein lies a cardinal fallacy common in critical discussions of *De L'Allemagne* and its influence. Mme de Staël does indeed present German literature as an essentially Romantic literature in contrast to the Classical heritage of France. In this she is following the distinction she had made in *De la littérature* between the literatures of the North and those of the South. Germany clearly belongs to the North with its aura of mists, melancholy, chivalry, in short the paraphernalia of Romanticism. This does not mean, however, that Mme de Staël actually writes about the German Romantic poets and thinkers. A glance at the contents of Part II ('De la littérature et des arts') of *De L'Allemagne* confirms this contention: there are sections on Wieland, Klopstock, Lessing, Winckelmann, Goethe, Schiller, and Herder as well as separate appraisals of Goethe's and Schiller's main plays. Other writers discussed in some detail include Bürger, Kotzebue, Klinger, Matthias Claudius, Iffland, Voss, Jacobi, Matthison, Tieck, Jean-Paul, Zacharias Werner and August Wilhelm Schlegel. With the exception of the last four, these are *not* the German Romantics. It becomes increasingly apparent on close analysis that while *De L'Allemagne* gives excellent coverage to various facets of the *Sturm und Drang*, it hardly touches the fringe of German Romanticism. The major poets of the *Frühromantik*, Novalis and Wackenroder, are not even mentioned in her survey of German literature, although reference is made to Novalis as a mystical thinker in Part IV (under the heading 'La religion et l'enthousiasme'). Nor is there any true appreciation of Friedrich Schlegel's significance as an aesthetician and experimenter.

It can of course be argued that the *Sturm und Drang* represents a pre-figuration of Romanticism. The line of continuity between the two movements is very evident in their rejection of the *status quo*, their common thrust towards a creative renewal of imaginative writing, their emphasis on the subjective, and their aesthetic credo of freedom in self-expression. But it would be wrong to overlook the differences, and simply to equate the *Sturm und Drang* with Romanticism. The *Sturm und Drang's* preoccupation with immediate social problems as against the inward orientation of Romanticism with its primacy of the imagination; the political aims of the *Stürmer und Dränger* in their assertion of liberty in contrast to the Romantics' mystical tendencies and metaphysical inclinations; the preference in the *Sturm und Drang* for drama as opposed to the *Roman* in all its variants favoured by the *Frühromantiker*: these differences go beyond a mere matter of intensity; they are sufficiently deep to give rise to a really fallacious picture when the *Sturm und Drang* is taken for Romanticism, as Mme de Staël did.

Her treatment of German prose fiction in *De L'Allemagne* can serve as a concrete example of the misleading effect of her fusion of the two movements. Prose fiction was not only the genre to which the *Frühromantiker* gave the greatest importance, but also that in which they were the most innovative. Of this Mme de Staël conveys little or no inkling. Even though she significantly advanced French acquaintance with German prose fiction, her coverage of this vital segment nonetheless has severe limitations, and shows beyond dispute that she did not in fact introduce the salient works of German Romanticism into France.

Of the thirty-two sections that make up Part II of *De L'Allemagne* only one (xxviii) treats the narrative, whereas no less than thirteen deal with drama, and five with lyric poetry. The imbalance within the section 'Des romans' is equally serious. After a peremptory dismissal of the many love-stories published in Germany, Mme de Staël devotes almost half of the section to Goethe. *Werther* is praised as 'sans égal et sans pareil'[8] ('unequalled and unparallelled'), an example of Goethe's genius at its most passionate. For this novel, already popular at the time when she was writing, Mme de Staël shows a deep understanding; as its two cardinal features, she underlines first Goethe's portrayal of 'les maladies de l'imagination de notre siècle' ('the ills of the imagination in our century' – iii, 248), and secondly the letter form, appealing to her age in its focus on inner feelings rather than outer happenings. Thus, in a couple of brief paragraphs, Mme de Staël has shrewdly brought out the historical importance of *Werther*. Goethe's other novels, however, fare less well: *Wilhelm Meister*, 'plein de discussions ingénieuses et spirituelles' ('full of clever and sprightly discussions' – iii, 252) that overshadow an uninteresting, quasi-superfluous hero, is deemed not 'très-attachant' ('very engaging' – iii, 258) with the exception of the beautiful episode of Mignon that won Mme de Staël's heart and that is recounted in some detail. Of *Die Wahlverwandtschaften* she is highly critical, faulting the novel's pessimistic implications, its avoidance of overt emotion, and above all, what she terms its vacillating stance, which she contrasts with the 'confiance' and 'enthousiasme' (iii, 266) that a work of art should inspire. This is a clear example of her rejection of a work because it did not fulfil *her* expectations of the novel. Tieck's *Sternbald*, on the other hand, is most sympathetically reviewed; here, as with *Werther*, Mme de Staël is astute, indeed daring, in her appreciation of its imaginative, poetic organisation. After a brief tribute to Claudius, the last third of the chapter consists of an attempt to assess Jean-Paul Richter. Though intrigued by 'des productions si extraordinaires' ('such extraordinary works' – iii, 274), Mme de Staël is at a loss for anything other than a paradoxical judgement: she praises the 'beautés admirables', the 'finesse', the 'gaieté' (iii, 276), the originality of his genius, but to her 'l'ordonnance et le cadre de ses tableaux sont si défectueux, que les traits de génie les plus lumineux se perdent dans la confusion de l'ensemble' ('the disposition and the framework of his pictures is so faulty that the brightest strokes of genius are lost in the confusedness of the whole' – iii, 276). She is obviously disorientated by Jean-Paul's writing and unable to place him within her experience or conception of the novel. Yet it is a measure of her fascination with Jean-Paul's 'sombre talent' (iii, 289) that she not only summarises two episodes (that of Lord Horion and his son from the beginning of *Hesperus*, and from *Titan* Emmanuel's description of the sunset), but also risks 'la traduction d'un morceau très-bizarre' ('the translation of a highly bizarre piece' – iii, 284), the so-called 'Songe', the first piece of the *Blumen-Frucht- und Dornenstücke*. And there, apart from a passing mention of August Lafontaine, the section 'Des romans' ends, with the tantalising remark: 'On n'en finirait point, si l'on voulait analyser la foule de romans spirituels et touchants que l'Allemagne possède' ('One would never finish if one wanted to analyse the host of clever and moving novels that Germany has'); the study of these novels would surely inspire 'le mouvement d'émulation' ('the urge to emulate' – iii, 290).

Faced with this teasing conclusion, the contemporary French reader of *De L'Allemagne* might well have wished for more. His curiosity would certainly have been aroused about German prose fiction, yet after a few pages he is left with an appetite whetted but unsatisfied. For when we ask dispassionately, how adequate is 'Des romans' as a presentation of German prose fiction at the turn of the century, the answer must be largely in the negative. In spite of Mme de Staël's pioneering exploration and her penetrating insight at various points, taken as a whole, as an introduction to German prose fiction, this section of *De L'Allemagne* is disappointingly scant. While it would be unfair to expect a comprehensive survey of the field, nevertheless the ommissions are numerous and glaring. The outstanding narratives of the *Frühromantik* – Friedrich Schlegel's *Lucinde*, Wackenroder's *Herzensergiessungen eines kunstliebenden Klosterbruders*, Novalis' *Heinrich von Ofterdingen*, the *Märchen* as a genre – all these are totally withheld from the French reader.

In the face of this textual evidence, it is time to revise the accepted view of *De L'Allemagne* as the work that brought German Romanticism into France. Mme de Staël herself is to some extent responsible for this misconception in that she presented the literature of Germany to her readers as an essentially Romantic literature in antithesis to the Classical heritage of France. In a wider sense this may be true, insofar as Germany's tradition tended towards irrationalism. But in the specific literary meaning, as pertaining to the Romantic movement of the late 1790s and early 1800s, the assumption must be refuted. Even the editors of the critical edition of *De L'Allemagne*, staunch *Staëliens* though they are, concede that 'Sous le nom de "Nouvelle école" elle mélange constamment le *Sturm und Drang*, le *Classicisme* et le *Romantisme* naissant' ('Under the name of "New School" she constantly mingles *Sturm und Drang*, *Classicism* and nascent

Romanticism' –ii, 41). In that mixture the *Sturm und Drang* was the dominant element. The aesthetic that emerges from Mme de Staël's account of German literature is unmistakably that of the *Sturm und Drang*. Repeatedly throughout *De L'Allemagne*, *De la littérature*, the *Carnets de voyage* and her letters the prime emphasis is on enthusiasm which she, like the *Stürmer und Dränger*, glorifies as the salient, divine quality of the genius. Mme de Staël subscribes to the *Sturm und Drang* conception of art as a spontaneous outpouring of enthusiasm. On the other hand, she does not share the German Romantics' preoccupation with the transcendental dimension, i.e. the transforming power of the imagination and the elevation of art to a religion. She appears to have had little awareness of the crucial importance of these facets when she impetuously presented – or rather, misrepresented – the *Sturm und Drang* as German Romanticism. But as a result of the picture proffered in *De L'Allemagne*, it was the *Sturm und Drang* that came for long to be regarded in France as German Romanticism, much to the detriment of the *Frühromantik* that was overlooked and neglected.

★   ★   ★   ★   ★

How did this substitution of the *Sturm und Drang* for Romanticism come about? It was certainly not the outcome of ignorance on Mme de Staël's part. Though it has been argued[9] that the book was dated even on its publication, springing as it did from impressions gathered some ten years earlier, there is little to suggest that this holds true for the sections on literature which appear to have been thoroughly re-worked in 1809.[10] One of her collaborators then was August Wilhelm Schlegel, for years her close friend and tutor to her children, from whom she would surely have heard of the most recent German writing. With Friedrich Schlegel, whom she had met in Berlin, she corresponded: he gave her three volumes of *Athenäum* and his novel, *Lucinde*. She also had works by Novalis, Schelling, Schleiermacher, Tieck, Chamisso, Jean-Paul, Fouqué, Fichte, Werner, and Wackenroder, in fact a good repertoire of German Romantic literature in her library at Coppet.[11] So it is in real puzzlement that one comes to investigate the reasons for her omission of the *Frühromantik* in favour of the *Sturm und Drang*.

The cause would seem to lie in a complex of outer and inner

factors: the genesis and intent of *De L'Allemagne*; Mme de Staël's working method; her language problems; her own background, personality and prejudices. All these combined to make *De L'Allemagne* what it is: a misleading intermediary.

To take first the outer factors. It is well to bear in mind that *De L'Allemagne* was not originally and primarily a book about literature; indeed, it came to be written almost by chance. Prior to 1803, oriented rather toward England or Italy, Mme de Staël had shown little interest in Germany. The sections of *De la littérature* that deal with Germany betray her scant acquaintance with the country and its literature at that time. She had read *Werther*, but when Goethe sent her a copy of *Wilhelm Meister* in 1797 she could only admire its binding! Between 1800 and 1803 she took a few German lessons, met some *émigrés* recently returned from Germany, as well as Charles Villers, who had published a series of articles on German literature and thought. But by and large she may be said to have shared the contemporary French indifference to Germany. Nor was her journey in 1803–4 inspired by any thirst for knowledge. It was not of her own volition as a learned investigator, but as an exile banished by Napoleonic decree that she crossed the Rhine in November 1803, with reluctance, misgivings and hesitations. Her initial unfavourable impressions of the country, recorded in the recently published *Carnets de voyage*, gradually changed during her stay in Weimar, and it was there in February 1804 that she conceived the idea of a book to reveal Germany to the French. 'J'ai passé des jours si heureux dans ce séjour' [i.e. Weimar] 'que mon jugement sur tous les objets se ressent des impressions que j'y ai éprouvées.'[12] ('I have spent such happy days here' [i.e. Weimar] 'that my judgement of everything is affected by my impressions here.') With these words Mme de Staël virtually admits the idealising trend that increasingly overlaid her earlier contradictory view of Germany. This idealisation was quickly fused with her ulterior political motives to turn *De L'Allemagne* from its very inception into an act of opposition to Napoleon. Still burning with resentment against the tyrant, she wanted to portray Germany, by contrast with France, as the land of liberty. As Heine so astutely realised, 'Der Hass gegen den Kaiser ist die Seele dieses Buches *De L'Allemagne*, und obgleich sein Name nirgends darin genannt wird, sieht man doch, wie die Verfasserin bei jeder Zeile nach den Tuilerien schielt.'[13] ('Hatred of the

Emperor is at the heart of this book, *De L'Allemagne*, and although his name is nowhere mentioned, one sees nonetheless how the author has her eye on the Tuileries in every line.') The obvious parallel with Tactitus' *De Germania* has often been made. What has not so far been underlined is the effect of this political bias on Mme de Staël's literary predilections. Her emphasis on the freedom in Germany naturally drew her towards the *Sturm und Drang*, particularly the dramas of rebellion which supported the rights of the individual against a repressive social order. The ethos and aesthetics of the *Sturm und Drang* fitted perfectly into her picture of Germany as the home of political idealism. Her focus on the *Sturm und Drang* thus served her practical purpose far more readily than a portrayal of the *Frühromantik* with its metaphysical emphasis could have done.

But this may suggest a greater degree of deliberate choice on Mme de Staël's part than was actually the case. Reading accounts of her travels and of the genesis of *De L'Allemagne*, one is constantly struck by the haphazardness of the whole enterprise. Even the decision to go to Germany was a last-minute improvisation, prompted by her desire to see Villers, who was then in Metz. As for her study of German literature, it was unsystematic, to say the least. She was gifted with a lively mind, shrewd insight and an astonishingly perspicacious instinctive judgement, but nothing was more alien to her than the scholar's slow, patient gathering of information. She relied on conversations, often rapid reading, samples, extracts, or the reports of friends. Heine's description 'wie dieser Sturmwind in Weibskleidern durch unser ruhiges Deutschland fegte'[14] ('how this whirlwind in woman's clothing swept through our tranquil Germany') is more than a mere witticism. Whirlwind impressions, however, are not the soundest basis for a balanced assessment of a country and its literature. A fair amount was, indeed, left to chance: she met those writers who happened to cross her path, read those books that were thrust at her (as in the case of Jean-Paul, whose *Briefe und bevorstehender Lebenslauf* were given to her by Villers to read in her carriage on the way). In Weimar, where she spent four out of her six months in Germany, she tended to meet the older generation, the former *Stürmer und Dränger*. The timing of her subsequent visit to Berlin, a centre of the *Romantik*, was, as Christopher Herold has pointed out, 'unfortunate. Novalis was dead; Tieck was absent; Brentano, Arnim, and Hoffmann had not yet arrived; Kleist was there, but unknown; Schelling was teaching at Wurzburg, Schleiermacher at Halle, Hegel at Jena.'[15] This 'unfortunate' timing is in many ways typical, and revealing of her adventitious approach to her subject. There is ample evidence to support Monchoux's contention that 'le caprice de l'auteur est la principale loi de cet ouvrage décousu'[16] ('the author's caprices were the main guidelines to this disjointed work').

This capriciousness was to some extent determined and also furthered by Mme de Staël's linguistic shortcomings. In her attempt to grasp German literature she was handicapped by her inadequate command of the language. In spite of her German lessons – first from Gerlach, her children's tutor, and later from Wilhelm Humboldt – she could not converse in German with any ease. As Jacobi wrote to her in November 1803; 'il y a un mal auquel ni votre célébrité, ni votre beau génie, et bien encore moins mes bons offices ne sauraient rémédier: c'est que vous ne savez pas vous exprimer en allemand, et que nos gens de lettres ne savent pas s'exprimer en français'[17] ('there is one difficulty which neither your fame, nor your brilliance, much less my good offices could remove: that is, that you cannot express yourself in German, and our men of letters cannot express themselves in French'). It is hard to assess how serious a barrier this was because of the conflicting evidence. On the one hand, Schiller, overcoming his reluctance to speak French, wrote to Goethe that he had managed tolerably well.[18] On the other hand, Mme de Staël, referring to the same conversation, complained to her father that Schiller 'parle très difficilement le français'[19] ('speaks French with great difficulty'), while she reported to Villers: 'nous nous sommes déjà disputés sans savoir nos langues mutuelles'[20] ('we have already engaged in lively discussion without knowing each other's languages'). Her stay in Weimar is punctuated by repeated references to language problems. Wieland, for example, cautiously asked: 'Oserais-je vous demander, Madame, si Fichte parle assez facilement le français pour pouvoir s'entretenir avec vous sur des objets de spéculation?'[21] ('Might I venture to enquire, Madame, whether Fichte speaks French with sufficient ease to be able to discuss speculative topics with you?') – a pertinent question indeed. In January 1804 already she was recruiting Jacobi's assistance with these words: 'Votre esprit est si clair et votre connaissance du français si parfaite que vous achèverez pour moi tous les commencements d'idées dont j'ai la tête remplie'[22] ('Your mind is so clear and your knowledge of French so excellent that you will complete for me all the incipient ideas that fill my head'). Nor was Jacobi the only one to be pressed into service. With her customary ingenuity, Mme de Staël hit on the idea of using English, which she knew well, as the medium for her study of German thought when she met Henry Crabb Robinson. He was, as he put it, 'commanded . . . to draw up for her Dissertations on the new philosophy'; he adds that she 'paid me for the trouble in loud praise, and promises or threatens me (whatever you will) with incorporating them in her great work on the German nation and literature she is now writing.'[23] There is thus little doubt that, as she herself confessed in *De L'Allemagne* (ii, 93), it was only 'à travers l'obstacle des mots' ('across the obstacle of the words') that she gained access to German literature. The insidious effect of these problems of communication was to bring her closer to those most proficient in French, specifically Wieland, who could hardly be said to represent the newest and most interesting in the German literature of the turn of the century.

Nevertheless, these outer factors alone would not in themselves have sufficed to focus Mme de Staël's attention on the *Sturm und Drang*. At a decisive level, inner factors too come into play, namely her own preferences and prejudices, which recent scholarship, notably that of Roland Mortier,[24] André Monchoux,[25] and Robert de Luppé,[26] has shown to be more complex than was previously assumed. Mme de Staël has commonly been portrayed as the harbinger of Romanticism, the electrifying apostle of enthusiasm. While this popular image undoubtedly contains a good deal of truth, it is somewhat simplistic, and needs to be corrected by a consideration of other elements in her personality. In background and upbringing she was very clearly a product of the eighteenth century, 'l'héritière la plus intelligente et la plus fidèle de l'esprit des lumières'[27] ('the most intelligent and most faithful inheritrix of the spirit of the Enlightenment'), as Mortier has – with perhaps a touch of exaggeration – called her. Though disenchanted with the Neo-classical French heritage and, therefore, more open to new ideas than many of her compatriots, in the last resort she still retained a certain caution, indeed ambivalence. Robert de Luppé has even gone so far as to brand her a 'prisonnière du passé'[28] ('a prisoner of the past'), while Jean Gibelin maintains that 'il ne lui est pas possible de sortir des limites élargies du goût français'[29] ('she is not able to go beyond the expanded limits of French taste'). These statements seem to be an over-correction of the previous tendency to envisage Mme de Staël as wholly forward-looking. The truth lies between the extremes: she did espouse 'l'enthousiasme', she did welcome the freshness of German literature, and she did want to see some of its innovations introduced into France; on the other hand, she did not hesitate to criticise Germany for its lack of elegance and *bon goût*, nor was she averse to appeals to 'les anciens' in her literary judgements.

Her subconscious impregnation with French standards certainly affected her attitude to German Romanticism. Its radical break with traditional aesthetics and its experimentation with accepted forms were too outrageous for the child of the Enlightenment that lurked beneath her tempestuous surface. The amount as well as the nature of the innovations practised by the *Sturm und Drang* were more in consonance with her own inclinations and ideas than those of the *Frühromantik*. Genius and enthusiasm, the essential tenets of the *Sturm und Drang*, aroused a more positive response in Mme de Staël than the metaphysics and imagination fundamental to the *Frühromantik*. As Schiller commented to Goethe:

> ihr Naturell und Gefühl ist besser als ihre Metaphysik, und ihr schöner Verstand erhebt sich zu einem genialischen Vermögen. Sie will alles erklären, einsehen, ausmessen, sie statuiert nichts Dunkles, Unzugängliches, und wohin sie nicht mit ihrer Fackel leuchten kann, da ist nichts für sie vorhanden. Darum hat sie eine horrible Scheu vor der Idealphilosophie, welche nach ihrer Meinung zur Mystik und zum Aberglauben führt, und das ist eine Stickluft, wo sie umkommt.[30]

> (her instinct and feeling are better than her capacity for metaphysics, and her fine understanding reaches the level of genius. She wants to explain, grasp, measure everything; she admits nothing dark and impenetrable, and those areas that she cannot illuminate with her torch do not exist for her. For this reason she has a terrible repugnance to idealistic philosophy, which in her view leads to mysticism and superstition, and that is a fatally poisonous atmosphere for her).

This perceptive diagnosis is confirmed by Mme de Staël's letters
from Germany which abound in whimsical, faintly derogatory
references to the 'bizarre métaphysique'[31] in which Goethe,
Schiller and their circle were absorbed, and which was evidently
alien and suspect to her.

In prose fiction too, to return to our specific example, her
judgements show signs of being determined by her heritage. It is
in keeping with the Neoclassical ranking of genres to place
drama in prime position, lyric poetry second, and prose narrative
a poor third, as Mme de Staël does. Some of her comments hint
at a certain contempt for the novel, specially for those features
which 'les anciens n'auraient jamais fait' ('the ancients would
never have done' – iii, 45). Her conception of the novel, as
Robert de Luppé has pointed out, stood clearly in the lineage of
Marmontel and La Harpe. Here, as in other parallel instances, her
literary conservatism is in striking contrast to her dynamic belief
in perfectibility. Her affiliations to the past made her wary of
extremes, particularly in regard to form. Goethe is reputed to
have faulted her lack of interest in form, while Heine called her
'die Sultanin des Gedankens'[32] ('the Sultana of thought') because
of her concentration on substance, idea and thought in preference
to shape. This mental bias of hers may help to explain her
avoidance of such works as *Lucinde, Heinrich von Ofterdingen* or
the *Herzensergiessungen*, all of which would no doubt have struck
her as too eccentric in form in contrast to the recognisable *roman
épistolaire, Werther,* and the picaresque outline of *Sternbald.*

Through her turn of mind then, as well as her background and
personality, Mme de Staël was thus more disposed to an innate
sympathy with the ideals of the *Sturm und Drang* than with those
of the *Frühromantik*. In these latent psychological and intellectual
inclinations, even more than in such outer factors as her ulterior
political motives and language problems, lie the deeper reasons
for her preference for the *Sturm und Drang.* It is as strange a
combination of circumstances as any in literary history that
brought the acceptance of the *Sturm und Drang* in France as
German Romanticism. Only the consequences of this misconception are as astonishing as its origins.

★   ★   ★   ★   ★

Mme de Staël's presentation of the *Sturm und Drang* as German
Romanticism had both immediate and lasting after-effects. *De*

L'Allemagne was immensely influential as an intermediary through its wide dissemination, its prodigious esteem and its almost unquestioned authority over many years. It was the standard primer for the French Romantics, few of whom knew enough German to attempt to read for themselves.[33] What is more, *De L'Allemagne* was instrumental in sending a whole chain of eminent Frenchmen – Quinet, Ampère, Michelet, Philarète Chasles, Xavier Marmier, Taine, Lerminier, Blaze de Bury, Saint-René Taillandier, to name only the most prominent – on pilgrimage to Germany. The extraordinary persistence of Mme de Staël's image of Germany is too well known and too fully documented to require any further elaboration.[34] Suffice it to say that the dissenting protests, such as those of Quinet, Heine, and Börne, were relatively sparse and little heeded. By and large, the vision of Germany projected by *De L'Allemagne* reigned supreme for a major part of the nineteenth century.

This holds true in the literary field too. Mme de Staël's views were accepted as virtually sacrosanct and her judgements repeated, often albeit in simplified fashion. Those German works and writers championed by her were the ones best received in France. The genres, periods and styles she recommended – the elegiac, the medieval, the Biblical – were adopted with alacrity. Goethe and Schiller were long – one might plausibly argue, still are – regarded in France as the foremost German Romantics. Again the fate of German prose fiction may serve as a paradigm. The continued dominance of Mme de Staël's preferences can be traced in the French reception of German prose for more than fifty years. *Werther*, for instance, the favourite of many of the French Romantics, completely overshadowed both *Wilhelm Meister* and *Die Wahlverwandtschaften*. Tieck's *Sternbald* was translated in 1823 by the baroness of Montolieu and was well received by *Le Globe* (iv [1828], and vii [1829]), the *Revue de Paris* (xliii [1841]) and the *Revue des Deux Mondes* (iv [1835]). The infiltration of Jean-Paul into France has been thoroughly traced by Claude Pichois who has shown that *bizarrerie*, Mme de Staël's term, became 'le leit-motiv des jugements sur Jean-Paul',[35] and who also maintains that the 'Songe', which she translated, was to haunt three generations of French poets and thinkers from Vigny, Michelet, Balzac and Hugo, through Musset, Gautier and Nerval, on to Baudelaire, Flaubert and Renan. Even August Lafontaine enjoyed considerable popularity: he was avidly read by Lamartine, and familiar to Stendhal and Balzac, who referred

to him (alongside *Faust!*) in *Eugénie Grandet*. The first more
systematic account of German literature, Loève-Weimars' *Résumé de l'histoire de la littérature allemande*, published in 1826, also
followed Mme de Staël closely in its choice and assessment of
writers, including for example Jean-Paul and Tieck, and exclud-
ing Friedrich Schlegel and Novalis. Thereby Mme de Staël's
image of German literature was further perpetuated.

The most serious consequences for the French in the long run
arose, however, less from Mme de Staël's pronouncements on
German literature than from her silences. Just as her judgements
re-echoed through the nineteenth century, so her omissions left
glaring gaps. Wackenroder, for instance, hardly receives any
mention other than a brief comment by Amédée Prévost in the
Revue de Paris (xliii [1841]) in an article on Tieck and his generation. Friedrich Schlegel, in line with Mme de Staël's approach, is
known as a thinker, an Orientalist and a Catholic, but of *Lucinde*
only a few fragments are translated and published in the *Nouvelle
Revue Germanique* (3 série, ii [1835]). Similarly Novalis, again in
accordance with Mme de Staël's projection, exists for the French
as the proponent of a kind of mystical scientific thought and not,
virtually until the end of the nineteenth century, as an imaginative poet.[36]

This adds up to more than a mere catalogue of certain German
writers known to the French in the nineteenth century and others
not known. What it means in the final analysis is that for most of
the century the French remained in ignorance of the *Frühromantik*. The *Hochromantik* – E. T. A. Hoffman, Heine, Uhland –
penetrated into France earlier and more easily to stand alongside
the *Sturm und Drang*. It was not until the middle of the century
that the poets of the *Frühromantik* began to infiltrate into France,
and it was really only the Symbolists who first appreciated the
full import of *Frühromantik* aesthetics. France awoke to the
Frühromantik through the intermediacy of Nerval, Baudelaire
and Wagner whose operas embodied Friedrich Schlegel's ideal of
a progressive universal poetry, as he called it in the 116th
Athenäum Fragment, in the form of the *Gesamtkunstwerk*. The
exaltation of the imagination as 'la reine des facultés'[37] ('the queen
of the faculties'), the systematic use of symbolic images as the
carriers of meaning, the delving into the mysteries of the subconscious, the stress on the musical, associative qualities of poetry:
all these aspects of the *Frühromantik* did not come into their own
in France until the Symbolist movement.

It would obviously be an exaggeration to ascribe to Mme de Staël the full responsibility for these literary developments, and even for certain political consequences, as Alexander Gillies tried to do when he maintained that the collapse of France in 1940 sprang ultimately from the intellectual confusion resulting from the 'series of legends' about Germany propagated by *De L'Allemagne*.[38] Nevertheless, the seeds of many strange features of Franco-German literary relations were undeniably sown in this intermediary that was at one and the same time so illuminating and so misleading. For *De L'Allemagne* set off a chain reaction. It stands at the fountain-head not only of a newly respectful attitude of the French towards their neighbours across the Rhine, but also of a perplexing time-lag of some fifty years between literary developments in the two countries. Just as the French Symbolists are the true counterparts to the German *Frühromantiker*, so French Romanticism corresponds in fact to the *Sturm und Drang*. In the primacy of enthusiasm, genius, freedom and spontaneity as the kernel of its aesthetics, in the unfettered drama of rebellion, in the emotional vehemence of its personal poetry, in the lyrical autobiographical novel, in the worship of nature, in the social involvement: in all these vital aspects French *romantisme* has a strong kinship to the *Sturm und Drang*. Though other forces inevitably came into play, Mme de Staël's establishment of the *Sturm und Drang qua* Romanticism in France was decisive in shaping the particular character of the French Romantic movement. Perhaps even more important in the long run was the corollary to her championship of the *Sturm und Drang*, namely her neglect of the *Frühromantik* which was thus effectively blocked from the consciousness of the French for half a century. Epoch-making though *De L'Allemagne* was as an intermediary, it was as much to mislead as to guide the nineteenth century.

NOTES TO CHAPTER 4

1. Johann Wolfgang von Goethe, *Sämtliche Werke*, (Stuttgart & Berlin: Cotta, 1903) vol. xxx, p. 134. Subsequent references are to this edition.
2. Claude Pichois, *L'Image de Jean-Paul Richter dans les lettres françaises* (Paris: Corti, 1963) p. 58.
3. J.-A. Bédé, in *Madame de Staël et l'Europe* (Paris: Klincksieck, 1970) p. 375.
4. Louis Belmontet, *Ode*, in *Mercure de France au XIXième siècle*, xx (1828) 497.

5. Peter L. Thorslev, Jr., *The Byronic Hero* (Minneapolis: Univ. of Minnesota Press, 1962) p. 191.

6. André Monchoux, 'La Place de Madame de Staël parmi les théoriciens du romantisme français', in *Madame de Staël et l'Europe*, p. 365.

7. J. Christopher Herold, *Mistress to an Age* (London: Hamilton, 1959).

8. Madame de Staël, *De L'Allemagne*, ed. Jean de Pange and Simone Balayé (Paris: Hachette, 1958–60) vol. iii, p. 246. Subsequent references are to this edition.

9. See Ernst Behler, 'Madame de Staël à Weimar 1803–1804', *Studi Francesi,* xxxvii (January–April 1969) 70.

10. See Jean de Pange, Introduction to *De L'Allemagne*, vol, i, p. xxiii.

11. For a catalogue of the German books in the library at Coppet see Jean de Pange, *Auguste-Guillaume Schlegel et Madame de Staël* (Paris: Albert, 1938) pp. 567–77.

12. *Les Carnets de voyage de Madame de Staël*, ed. Simone Balayé (Geneva: Droz, 1971) p. 69.

13. Heinrich Heine, *Sämtliche Werke*, ed. E. Elster (Leipzig and Vienna: Bibliographisches Institut, n.d.) vol. vi, pp. 25–6.

14. Heine, *Sämtliche Werke*, vol. vi, p. 25.

15. Herold, *Mistress to an Age*, p. 269.

16. André Monchoux, *L'Allemagne devant les lettres françaises 1814–1835* (Toulouse: Colin, 1953) p. 10.

17. Madame de Staël, *Choix de lettres, 1778–1817*, ed. Georges Solovieff (Paris: Klincksieck, 1970) p. 245.

18. Schiller, Letter of 21 December 1803 to Goethe, in *Sämtliche Werke*, vol. xxxi, p. 126.

19. 25 December 1803, Mme de Staël, *Choix de lettres*, p. 242.

20. 15 December 1803; quoted by Jean de Pange, *Madame de Staël et la découverte de l'Allemagne* (Paris: Malfère, 1928) p. 36.

21. 8 April 1804; quoted by Jean de Pange, *Madame de Staël et la découverte de l'Allemagne*, p. 50.

22. Mme de Staël, *Choix de lettres*, p. 246.

23. Unpublished letter of Henry Crabb Robinson to his brother, written late March 1804; quoted in Jean-Marie Carré, 'Madame de Staël et Henry Crabb Robinson', *Revue de l'histoire littéraire*, xix (1912) 541.

24. Roland Mortier, 'Madame de Staël et l'héritage des "Lumières"', *Madame de Staël et l'Europe*, pp. 129–39.

25. Monchoux, 'La Place de Madame de Staël parmi les théoriciens du romantisme français', in *Madame de Staël et l'Europe*, pp. 261–376.

26. Robert de Luppé, *Les Idées littéraires de Madame de Staël et l'héritage des lumières 1795–1800* (Paris: Vrin, 1969).

27. Mortier, 'Madame de Staël et l'héritage des "Lumières"', in *Madame de Staël et l'Europe*, p. 129.

28. Luppé, *Les Idées littéraires de Madame de Staël et l'héritage des lumières*, p. 161.

29. Jean Gibelin, *L'Esthétique de Schelling et 'L'Allemagne' de Madame de Staël* (Paris: Champion, 1934), p. 77.

30. Goethe, *Sämtliche Werke*, vol. xxxi, p. 126.

31. 15 December 1803 to her father, Mme de Staël. *Choix de lettres*, p. 239.

32. Heine, *Sämtliche Werke*, vol. vi, p. 24.

33. See P. Lévy, 'Les Romantiques français et la langue allemande', *Revue Germanique*, xxix (1938) 225–52.

34. See Jean-Marie Carré, *Les Ecrivains français et le mirage allemand* (Paris: Boivin, 1947); André Monchoux, *L'Allemagne devant les lettres françaises 1814–1835* (Toulouse: Colin, 1953); Claude Digeon, *La Crise allemande de la pensée française* (Paris: Presses universitaires, 1959).

35. Pichois, *L'Image de Jean-Paul Richter dans les lettres françaises*, p. 54.

36. See Werner Vordtriede, *Novalis und die französischen Symbolisten* (Stuttgart: Kohlhammer, 1963).

37. Charles Baudelaire, *Curiosités esthétiques* (Paris: Garnier, 1962) p. 320.

38. Alexander Gillies, 'Some Thoughts on Comparative Literature', *Yearbook of Comparative and General Literature*, i (1952) 20–23.

5 Benjamin Constant's *Wallstein*

The night of 31 August 1807 witnessed a crisis unprecedented even in the tempestuous relationship of Benjamin Constant and Mme de Staël. Constant had finally decided to break loose in order to marry Charlotte du Tertre. In his *Journal Intime* of 30 August he notes: 'Mon parti est pris. . . . Je romps enfin'[1] ('I have made up my mind. . . . I am at last breaking loose'). Mme de Staël's reaction was characteristically violent; in the course of a frightful scene, amidst hysterical ravings, she staged a sham suicide which, however, prevented neither Constant from fleeing nor her from pursuing him. Once again Constant was unable to escape what he calls, in that same diary entry, her 'puissance magique qui me domine' ('her magic binding spell'). He records the events of that 'nuit convulsive' ('agitated night') with touching brevity: 'Elle est arrivée. Elle s'est jetée à mes pieds, elle a poussé des cris. Quel coeur de fer eût resisté?' ('She came. She threw herself at my feet, she cried out loud. What heart of steel could have resisted?' – 1 September 1807, p. 624). The break was thus postponed, and Constant returned to Coppet with the promise to stay for six weeks, until mid-October.

It was during those six weeks, during this more or less enforced sojourn at Coppet, that Constant began work on his *Wallstein.* The idea may have been suggested to him by Mme de Staël who had previously tried to apply this same 'favourite sedative'[2] to Narbonne in similar circumstances in 1800. There is little evidence of any earlier interest in *Wallenstein* on Constant's part. When he had met Schiller on several occasions in Weimar during his visit there in January and February 1804, he had been much less impressed by him than by Goethe; of his works only *Wilhelm Tell* was then singled out for special praise. But now he set to work with great gusto, mainly 'pour tuer le temps d'ici au

74

15 octobre' ('to kill the time between now and 15 October' – p. 624). The first mention of the plan for *Wallstein* comes on 4 September, and on the following days he rejoices in his rapid progress: 'Ma tragédie avance' ('my tragedy is making headway' – 6 September); 'bien. J'ai déjà fait 280 vers' ('good. I have already done 280 lines' – 7 September); 'Fait 328 vers' ('done 328 lines' – 8 September); 'j'en ai fait 454 vers' ('I have done 454 lines' – 9 September); 'le premier acte fini' ('the first act is finished' – 10 September, p. 625). Towards mid-September work was slowed down by further emotional upheavals, from which Constant found refuge in the play that 'm'occupe très agréablement' ('keeps me very pleasantly occupied' – 24 September, pp. 627–8) and 'me console de tout' ('comforts me well' – 26 September, p. 628). Constant never concealed either from himself or from others that this task was a flight from an uncongenial situation; as he wrote to Hochet on 10 September: 'Il a cet avantage, qu'il me sort plus qu'aucun autre du monde réel, et a moins de rapports qu'aucun autre avec les circonstances du moment'[3] ('Its great advantage is that it removes me more than anything else from the real world and has less connection than anything else with present circumstances'). By mid-September the work was progressing 'fort' ('well' – 21 September), even 'prodigieusement' ('prodigiously' – 23 September, p. 627), so that before the end of the month the second act was finished, and a week later the third too. The fourth act, though not quite as quick as the previous three, was done in the course of October, and it was only 'ce diable de cinquième acte' ('this devil of a fifth act' – 31 October, p. 634) that caused Constant any real difficulty. But 'ce maudit dernier acte' ('this cursed last act' – 5 November, p. 635) was in turn almost finished by the latter half of November when a sheet of Constant's *Journal* is missing so that the exact date of completion is unknown. It must have been early December 1807, for on the fifth of that month *Wallstein* made a private debut in Mme de Nassau's salon.

At its first public reading in Paris in February 1808 the play was not well received. Mme de Staël advised Constant to aim at publication rather than performance, and wisely urged him to add an explanatory preface. By mid-summer Constant had overcome his initial disappointment sufficiently to accept this advice. After renouncing hope of performance, he prepared the text for publication, aspiring at least to a *succès de librairie*. Finally in September 1808 the preface was finished and in January 1809 *Wallstein, tragédie en cinq actes et en vers, précédée de quelques réflexions sur le théâtre allemand, et suivie de notes historiques, par Benjamin Constant de Rebecque* was published by J. J. Paschoud of Paris and Geneva.

Wallstein created an immediate sensation. Within two months the first edition was sold out, and plans were under way for a reprint. On 20 February 1809 Mme de Staël reported to the Duchess of Saxony and Weimar: '*Wallstein* fait une grande sensation à Paris: c'est un événement littéraire: on se bat "pour" et "contre" avec acharnement'[4] ('*Wallstein* is causing a great sensation in Paris: it is a literary event: people are taking sides heatedly "for" and "against"'). By 12 March Constant himself wrote to his aunt: 'Si attirer l'attention du public est un succès pour un ouvrage, *Wallstein* a joui de ce succès, autant qu'il est possible. Il a été amèrement et, selon moi, injustement critiqué dans quelques journaux, et tolérablement défendu dans d'autres'[5] ('If attracting public attention is a sign of success for a work, then *Wallstein* has enjoyed this success to the greatest extent. It has been bitterly and, in my view, unjustly criticised in several journals and defended after a fashion in others'). The most hostile criticism came from the *Journal de Paris*, which devoted four articles (12, 13, 21 and 23 February 1809) to Constant's play, branding it a literary monstrosity. *Wallstein* was attacked as a cold, intellectual construction; a hybrid true neither to history nor to Schiller; a tragedy neither French nor German; a play that suffered from vagueness and obscurity, and whose characters understood their own conduct as little as did the audience.

Nor has Constant's work fared appreciably better in later criticism. The sketchy articles of E. Meyer[6] and K. R. Gallas[7] are both negative in their judgement; Edmond Eggli[8] has concentrated primarily on the sources of Constant's ideas, while Carlo Cordié[9] has collected information about the work's genesis and reception. It is only quite recently, in Jean-René Derré's critical edition,[10] that a serious attempt at a re-assessment has been made. At last the actual text has become readily available, together with various documents such as Prosper de Barante's previously unpublished commentary. Yet even Derré's introduction misses the long-term historical implications of Constant's work. Through his reiterated emphasis on Constant's ties to the French Neoclassical tradition, Derré fails to appreciate the full signifi-

cance of Constant's understanding of the basic differences between French and German drama. The importance of *Wallstein*
lies in the very contradiction between the timidity of Constant's
practices and his extraordinarily perspicacious insight into the
dilemma facing French dramatists. This paradox at one and the
same time reflects and reveals the intertwining of political and
literary issues in France at that time, so that an analysis of
Wallstein and its preface represents an exemplary case-study of
the historical situation.

★   ★   ★   ★   ★

Wallstein is, admittedly, indefensible either as an adaptation of
Schiller's *Wallenstein* or as a drama in its own right. It is hardly
fair even to measure it up against Schiller because Constant
clearly never intended it as a direct translation. In the preface he
states categorically that 'une traduction, ou même une imitation
exacte était impossible'[11] ('a translation, or even a precise imitation was impossible'); he concedes that 'il n'y a pas, dans les trois
tragédies de Schiller, une seule scène que j'ai conservée en entier'
('there is not, in Schiller's three plays, a single scene that I have
maintained in its entirety' – p. 60). Schiller's name does not
therefore figure at all on the title-page. From the outset Constant
refers to his work in his *Journaux Intimes* as 'ma tragédie' ('my
tragedy' – 5, 6, 9, 17, 19, 21, 23, 26 September 1807, pp. 624–8).
In a letter to Fauriel of 22 July 1808[12] he calls it 'une imitation très
libre' ('a very free imitation'), and this was the word he also used
twenty years later in his *Réflexions sur la tragédie*.[13] It is in fact an
appropriate term insofar as Constant's *Wallstein* is a tragedy
based on, and imitated from, Schiller's *Wallenstein*, rather than a
direct translation. As a translation it would be a ludicrous
travesty; as an adaptation, on the other hand, it is of considerable
interest, particularly in its departures from its model. Where,
how, and above all, why Constant modified his original is worth
detailed attention.

Schiller's mighty trilogy, sub-titled 'ein dramatisches Gedicht'
('a dramatic poem') is turned into a 'tragédie en cinq actes et en
vers' ('a verse tragedy in five acts'). The total length is drastically
cut from some 9000 lines in German to 2800 in French, and the
characters are reduced from twenty-two (not to mention the
crowds of *Wallensteins Lager*) in Schiller's trilogy to twelve and

some unidentified 'followers'. Several of the names have been changed, partly out of euphonious considerations and partly for the sake of assimilation to the French milieu: Octavio Piccolomini becomes the Count of Gallas and his son, Max, is re-named Alfred; Wrangel is called Harald, and Questenberg is turned into Géraldin. The countess Terzky, Wallenstein's wife, and more important, the astrologer, are suppressed completely. Schiller's prologue is omitted, as is the whole of *Wallensteins Lager* because 'il serait impossible de transporter sur notre théâtre cette singulière production de génie'[14] ('it would be impossible to transfer this singular creation of genius onto our stage'). Categoric though this assertion is, Constant gives no valid reasons to support it; his argument – the disorderliness of seventeenth-century armies – is evasive and unconvincing. It is indeed elsewhere that the grounds for this striking omission lie, namely in Constant's conception of French stage properties and expectations.

That is the heart of the matter. All the major changes made by Constant in adapting Schiller's trilogy are motivated by one and the same factor: his determination to squeeze the vast German historical drama into the bounds of the regular French Neoclassical form. The *Lager* was the first victim on the altar of the unities which Constant observed meticulously. 'J'ai écarté tout ce que rejettaient invinciblement les règles de notre art dramatique'[15] ('I have eliminated all that is wholly unacceptable to the rules of our theatre'), he wrote to Fauriel on 22 July 1808. Whereas Schiller's three plays span a considerable length of time, culminating in Wallenstein's death, all the action of the French version is concentrated on one day, 25 February 1634, the day of the assassination. Likewise the scene is confined to the palace at Eger, while Schiller moves freely from Pilsen to Eger. And because 'j'ai cru devoir observer les règles de notre théâtre, même dans un ouvrage déstiné à faire connaître le théâtre allemand, j'ai supprimé beaucoup de petits incidents'[16] ('I felt obliged to observe the rules of our theatre, even in a work intended to make the German theatre known, I have suppressed many small incidents'). Among the casualties is the generals' great feast, which fills the whole of the fourth act of *Die Piccolomini*, as well as the scene (*Wallensteins Tod*, act V, scene iv) in which Wallenstein recalls his youth and ironically looks forward to a brilliant future on the very brink of death and in the presence of the man who knows of the fate about to befall him. In each case Constant expresses his regret, but in each case he has ruthlessly deleted dramatic high-points. It must, however, be said that Constant's contemporaries were wholeheartedly in favour of these amendments. Representative of their attitude is Jean-Louis Laya's opinion 'qu'on ne peut qu'approuver la plupart de ses changements et surtout de ses sacrifices'[17] ('one cannot but approve of the majority of his changes and specially of his cuts').

Far more serious than these restrictions and suppressions is the overall weakening of the dramatic effect resulting from Constant's submission to standard Neoclassical usage. He tends, for instance, to replace Schiller's direct action on stage by the customary *récit*, which was specifically designed to avoid any such visible action. In his preface Constant admits the shortcomings of this practice: 'L'obligation de mettre en récit ce que, sur d'autres théâtres, on pourrait mettre en action, est un écueil dangereux pour les tragiques français'[18] ('the need to convey by narrative what could, on other stages, be shown by action is a danger for French tragedians'). Yet paradoxically, or rather, characteristically, he does not depart from the accepted conventions of his age. The dramatic tension is lessened appreciably when *récit* replaces the live portrayal of Wallenstein's personal authority in the *Lager* and again in the scene (*Wallensteins Tod*, act III, scene xv) where the impact of his presence alone quells the troops' threatened rebellion. Such reduction from dynamic drama to mere telling is apparent throughout, and the impression of bookishness is enhanced by Constant's copious historical notes, some of which were actually translated from Schiller's scholarly work on the Thirty Years' War. There are many examples of the weakening of the dramatic effect. The method is the same in each instance: the forceful bluntness of the German is attenuated into an innocuous smoothness in compliance with French standards of seemliness. Yet – perhaps ironically – this does not preclude a certain melodramatic colouring wholly absent in Schiller. Nowhere is the divergence between the German drama and the French imitation more evident than in the closing scenes. The verbosity of Isolan's *récit* of Wallstein's assassination and the sentimentality of the weeping Thécla are in sharp contrast to the stark horror of Schiller's climax. The ominous silence of the night is suddenly broken as the house is thrown into disarray by news of the bloody deed. And the trilogy ends with a masterly stroke as the imperial seal is handed to 'Dem Fürsten Piccolomini' ('Prince Piccolomini'). Compared to this stunning bang, the tears of Constant's Thécla are just a whimper.

So as to achieve the clarity of outline demanded by French Neoclassicism Constant had to simplify the German play very considerably. French tragedy, he rightly recognised,[19] prefers the anatomy of a single passion to the panorama of a whole life given by the Germans. The French, therefore, tended to avoid contradictions, such as the contiguity of good and evil. In order to conform to this tradition Constant had to strip the central figure of many of his complexities. That Constant fully appreciated the psychological subtleties of Schiller's portrayal is shown by his shrewd analysis in the preface.[20] Nevertheless, the strong claims of convention overruled his intellectual perception, as in his use of *récit*. Constant's Wallstein is neither tortured by doubts and hesitations nor moved by irrational motives; his deceptive dream about Octavio Piccolomini is quashed, along with the figure of the astrologer, so that little remains of his profound faith in the stars. The intriguing twilight surrounding Schiller's puzzling Wallenstein is changed by Constant into clear-cut black and white. From the beginning Wallstein is presented as a villain, with the result that Géraldin can summarily dismiss Gallas' scruples about betraying him. The disagreements between Wallstein and the Imperial Court are so far minimised as to seem mere trifles, while the larger political issues are entirely ignored. Wallstein is so thoroughly blackened by Constant that there can be no doubt as to his guilt; it is he who suggests the trick with the generals' signature in ignoble conspiracy with Illo. Wallstein degenerates even further as the play progresses. The very truncated version of his great monologue[21] is indicative of Constant's scant interest in the psychological motivation as well as of the loss of that grandeur and dignity that distinguishes Schiller's hero. Towards the close of Constant's play Wallstein is no more than a base opportunist, putting on a show of patriotic bravado, and anxious to find a scapegoat as the tide turns against him.

Yet even this flattened character provoked criticism of a kind that is highly revealing of the climate of opinion in early nineteenth-century France. In spite of Constant's attenuation of the irrational elements, Jean-Louis Laya launched a vehement attack on Wallstein's superstition: 'C'est un étrange langage sans doute que celüi-ci dans la bouche d'un conspirateur'[22] ('This is strange language indeed in the mouth of a conspirator'). The 'strange language' to which he took exception includes such words as 'mystérieux' ('mysterious') and 'interroger le sort' ('question fate') in Wallstein's speech in act III, scene i. Laya concludes that a leader so visionary by temperament ('son caractère d'illuminé') was bound to come to grief. It was such criticism from his contemporaries that Constant recalled years later in his 1829 *Réflexions sur la tragédie*.[23] However insipid Wallstein may seem to us, to the French of that time he was still outrageously non-conformist, notwithstanding Constant's efforts to avoid offence to native conventions.

Like Wallstein, the other characters too are compounded of milk and water rather than the blood and thunder of the German trilogy. This is particularly true of Alfred, who does not stand comparison with the impetuous, independent Max Piccolomini, the very incarnation of idealism in all its innocence. Beside him Alfred is a puppet, spouting oratorial inanities. Even more infelicitous is the treatment of Thécla, who proved most troublesome to Constant. Realising that the forthright German girl would not meet with the approval of a French audience, he wrote about her at length in his preface.[24] What would shock the French was acceptable to the Germans, he explains, because of the differing evaluation of love in the two countries! So, in accordance with his usual practice, Constant aimed at compromise, tailoring her to French 'proportions', as he puts it, while trying to maintain something of the German flavour. In fact, the French Thécla is not only saddled with the customary confidant; she is turned into a frivolous creature, wholly lacking the boldness of Schiller's Thekla. The glaring disparity between the bearing of Schiller's characters and that of their French equivalents becomes immediately evident in Thécla's first meeting with her father.

This encounter of father and daughter, like the narrative of Wallstein's death, reveals another flaw in Constant's tragedy: a certain tendency to sentimentality. This stems in large measure from Constant's uncritical adoption of the stock-in-trade vocabulary of French Neoclassical drama. Throughout, the style is extremely laboured, often long-winded, stilted, precious, and riddled with periphrasis. It is indeed stagey language of the worst kind, in contrast to Schiller's lively, natural dialogue with its jagged exclamations, impatient interjections and vigorous, realistic expressions. The vivid, terse repartee of the German is replaced by lengthy pieces of oratory in French. The discrepancy in style is most apparent where Constant has remained closest to the original. Thus Wallenstein's simple, poignant phrase (*Wallensteins Tod*, act II, acene iii):

> Es gibt im Menschenleben Augenblicke,
> Wo er dem Weltgeist näher ist, als sonst,
> Und eine Frage frei hat an das Schicksal.

is rendered by this piece of word–embroidery:

> Il est, pour les mortels, des jours mystérieux,
> Où, des liens du corps, notre âme dégagée,
> Au sein de l'avenir est tout à coup plongée,
> Et saisit, je ne sais par quel heureux effort,
> Le droit inattendu d'interroger le sort,[25]

Constant does attempt to excuse his verse by his repeated insistence in the preface on the difficulties of the Alexandrine, which demands 'des circonlocutions continuelles'[26] ('constant circumlocutions') and 'une certaine noblesse soutenue'[27] ('certain sustained nobility'). Moreover, since common speech was inadmissible in high tragedy, some scenes had to be excluded, notably those in which rough soldiers appeared – which again helps to account for the suppression of the *Lager*. In his use of the Alexandrine and in his shunning of the commonplace Constant was once more bowing to tradition.

As it stands, spineless and colourless, *Wallstein* is hardly a shadow of Schiller's trilogy. Constant disregarded many vital aspects of his German model: the essential element of mystery in Wallenstein's character and actions; the unconscious forces shaping the events; the contrast between Wallenstein and Max; Wallenstein's special relationship to both the army and his daughter. Those scenes that Constant himself invented and added (act I, scene iii, and act V, scenes i and ii) further underline his lack of understanding through their sheer incongruity. Even Mme de Staël, who praised *Wallstein* so lavishly and staunchly countered most criticisms, finally conceded that the work would have been more 'curieux, si l'auteur français ne s'était pas si rigoureusement asservi à la régularité française'[28] ('remarkable, if the French author had not submitted so strictly to French regularity'). It is not surprising that this version was superseded by the translation of Charles Liadières, which was performed at the *Théâtre français* on 22 November 1828; it was closer to the German and more effective dramatically.

★   ★   ★   ★   ★

While *Wallstein* as a play is at best a curiosity, its preface is of great historical importance. The addition of *Quelques réflexions sur le théâtre allemand* was originally motivated, in part at least, by political considerations; Constant was not in favour with the Imperial government, and the theme of *Wallstein* – rebellion against an emperor – might well have seemed seditious. Constant felt little enthusiasm about the writing of the preface; he confided to Fauriel on 15 September 1808:

> Je suis actuellement occupé à faire un petit Discours préliminaire dans lequel je ne ferais pas, à beaucoup près, la comparaison de l'art dramatique allemand et du nôtre, comme vous semblez vous y attendre. Ce n'est pas que je ne trouve moi-même que ce serait la place et l'occasion d'un pareil travail. Mais je suis mal disposé, pressé de publier, parce que je voudrais en avoir fini de cette entreprise, qui m'a détourné plus long temps que je ne voulais de mon ouvrage sur le *Polythéisme.*[29]

> (I am at the moment engaged on a small Preface in which I shall not, by any means, set up a comparison between German dramatic art and ours, as you seem to expect. It is not that I, for my part, do not consider this to be the place and the occasion for such a comparison. But I am little inclined to do it, being in haste to publish because I would like to be finished with this undertaking which has diverted me longer than I wished from my work on *Polytheism.*)

In spite of Constant's scepticism and avowed haste, the preface turned out better than he anticipated. It proved less a political apologia than a defence of his adaptation. And his attempt to justify what he had done throws much light on dramatic practices and opinions in France at that time.

After outlining the significance of the Thirty Years' War in German history and Wallenstein's role in it, Constant gives a brief sketch of Schiller's trilogy as a preliminary to the analysis of his own play. His apologia is based on a frank discussion of the difficulties that had faced him. The first was obviously the very length of Schiller's work which comprises, according to Constant, a play without action (*Wallensteins Lager*), an action without a denouement (*Die Piccolomini*), and finally a denouement without an exposition (*Wallensteins Tod*). It was Constant's resolve from the outset to compress the three into a single drama. The problem of length was, thus, acute, and it was compounded by Constant's commitment to the long verse-form of the Alexandrine. The second obstacle lay in the subject-matter, not only in its unfamiliarity to the French, but also in its departure from the habit of drawing material from Classical antiquity. The third and most serious difficulty resided in the familiar tone of the German dialogue. For, Constant explains,

> la langue de la tragédie allemande n'est point astreinte à des règles aussi délicates, aussi dédaigneuses que la nôtre. La pompe inséparable des Alexandrins nécessite dans l'expression une certaine noblesse soutenue. Les auteurs Allemands peuvent employer, pour le développement des caractères, une quantité de circonstances accessoires qu'il serait impossible de mettre sur notre théâtre sans déroger à la dignité requise: et cependant ces petites circonstances répandent dans le tableau présenté de la sorte beaucoup de vie et de vérité.[30]

> (the language of German tragedy is not governed by the same standards of delicacy and refinement as ours. The innate grandeur of the Alexandrine demands a certain sustained nobility of expression. German authors can use all sorts of attendant details in the development of character which would be impossible on our stage without detracting from the required dignity; yet these little details give life and beauty to the picture).

Constant cites examples of such homely realism in Goethe's *Götz von Berlichingen* and Schiller's *Jungfrau von Orleans*, but he concludes: 'Aucune tournure poétique ne permettrait de transporter ce détail sur notre théâtre: l'emphase des paroles ne ferait que gâter le naturel de la situation, et ce qui est touchant en Allemand, ne serait en Français que ridicule'[31] ('No poetic turn of phrase could make such detail permissible in our theatre: the pomp of the language would only spoil the naturalness of the situation, so that what is touching in German would merely be ridiculous in French'). Constant here shows a real understanding of German drama, and above all of its fundamental divergence from the French Neoclassical tradition. But he accepts the *status quo* in France even though this forces him to radical changes and cuts in Schiller's play. Thus, after defending his treatment of Wallstein and of Thécla, he ends on a blandly conciliatory note by lauding the unquestionable superiority of French tragedy, yet at the same time issuing a warning against narrow-minded disdain of other nations.

Constant's apologia for his actual practices is less important than the wider reflections that arise out of his consideration of specific points of difficulty. His inductive approach, moving from the particular to the general, lends substance and conviction to his ideas. As a critic Constant has sensitivity, breadth of vision and intellectual acuity, as is shown by his appreciation of the dramatic force of *Wallenstein* and of other German plays.

Contrary to his disclaimer in that letter to Fauriel of 15 September 1808, perhaps even against his own intentions, Constant does make a comparison of the German and French approach in drama. He is able to discern a number of cardinal differences. First, the German theatre is more realistic in its action, as his examples from *Götz von Berlichingen* and *Die Jungfrau von Orleans* illustrate. Allied to this realism in action is a greater naturalness and freedom in both language and versification. The same flexibility is evident also in the secondary characters, who may either assume the function of the Greek chorus, or heighten the theatrical effect through contrast, as in Schiller's *Wilhelm Tell* when a wedding procession crosses Tell's path as he lies in wait to kill the tyrant Gessler. Repeatedly the emphasis falls on the greater freedom of German drama. Constant attributes the dichotomy between French and German tragedy to the ultimate contrast in their conception of the scope and range of the genre: 'Les Français, même dans celles de leurs tragédies qui sont fondées sur la tradition ou sur l'histoire, ne peignent qu'un fait ou une passion. Les Allemands, dans les leurs, peignent une vie entière et un caractère entier'[32] ('The French, even in those of their tragedies that are based on tradition or history, depict only one event or one passion. The Germans paint a whole life and a whole character'). So the Germans are at liberty not only to present a full biography in dramatic form but also, like the English, to portray a character in all his complexity, even contradictoriness. This expansiveness is the opposite of the French concentration that can lead to excessive simplification and to formalised stereotypes. What, asks Constant, do we know of Phèdre or of Andromaque beyond their one dominant passion? In a letter to Barante of 25 February 1808 he complains of the limited number of 'moules à caractère' ('character moulds') possible in the French theatre, adding not without bitterness: 'Ce ne sont pas les hommes qu'il faut peindre, mais des cadres donnés à remplir'[33] ('It is not a matter of depicting men, but of filling in outlines'). The disparity between Schiller's rounded Wallenstein and Constant's flat Wallstein in fact illustrates the distinction made in the preface between the German preference for individuality and the French insistence on homogeneity.

In spite of his perspicacious grasp of the differences between the French and the German manner, Constant is extremely cautious in regard to any changes the French could or should make. He states categorically: 'Je suis loin de recommander l'introduction de ces moyens dans nos tragédies. L'imitation des tragiques allemands me semblerait très dangereuse pour les tragiques français'[34] ('I am far from recommending the introduction of these modes in our tragedies. The imitation of the German tragedians would seem to me very dangerous for the French'). The dangers he fears are those of excess and exaggeration, and a glance at subsequent French Romantic melodrama shows that his anxieties were by no means unfounded. Constant even goes so far as to attempt a defence of the unities as a wise law ('une loi sage'[35]), but he does so without much spirit or conviction. This is hardly surprising in view of Constant's precarious stance in the preface. Throughout he is endeavouring to maintain an uneasy balance between his conservative inclinations on the one hand, and on the other his intellectual recognition of the need to revitalise French drama. He was himself painfully aware of the ambiguity of his position. The equivocations of the preface to *Wallstein* clearly offer an example of that timidity for which Constant has so often been criticised. 'Je ne veux point proposer d'innovations à mes risques et périls, et de toutes les réputations celle que j'aimerais le moins serait celle d'un novateur'[36] ('I do not want to propose innovations at my risk and peril, and the reputation I would like least is that of innovator'), he wrote to Barante on 23 November 1808. Even twenty years later, in his *Réflexions sur la tragédie*, Constant still felt the need to justify himself: 'Je m'exprimais toutefois avec discrétion et avec réserve. J'ai toujours eu de la répugnance pour toutes les innovations violentes'[37] ('I expressed myself with prudence and restraint. I have always felt repugnance to violent innovations'). Constant's dislike of revolutionary change would certainly have prevented him from suggesting the abandonment of the Neoclassical rules. Nevertheless, the 1809 preface to *Wallstein* was of major importance for the clear distinction it drew between the French and the German approaches in drama, as well as for its intelligent appraisal of a foreign system.

Constant was rather less cautious in the revised version of the preface published in 1829 under the title *De la Guerre de Trente Ans, de la Tragédie de Wallstein par Schiller, et du Théâtre Allemand*. In substance this second text is largely similar to that of 1809; much of it, specially the beginning, is a literal repetition of the earlier version with some slight rearrangements. Constant's purpose, however, has changed: while he was aiming in 1809 to justify his procedures, by 1829 he seeks to answer criticisms of *Wallstein* and to examine its flaws. These he often admits with a disarming candour; for instance, he acknowledges his mistakes in his portrayal of Thécla and in his use of *récit*, particularly for the exposition of Wallstein's character. He now omits not only his defence of the unities, but also his previous refusal to recommend the introduction of German methods into the French theatre. Indeed, he even goes so far as to acknowledge that 'en me condamnant à respecter toutes les règles de notre théâtre, j'avais détruit, de plusieurs manières, l'effet dramatique.'[38] ('in forcing myself to observe all the rules of our theatre, I ruined the play's dramatic effect in various respects.')

It is in its ending that the 1829 text departs most strikingly from the earlier version. Instead of closing with a short and conciliatory paragraph, as he had done in 1809, Constant now observes: 'Plus prévoyant, ou plus hardi, j'aurais évité la plupart des fautes que je viens d'indiquer dans mon propre ouvrage. J'aurais dû pressentir qu'une révolution politique entraînerait une révolution littéraire'[39] ('If I had had more foresight, or been bolder, I would have avoided most of the flaws I have just pointed out in my own work. I should have intuited that a political revolution would bring a literary revolution in its wake'). Looking back from the vantage-point of 1829, Constant lays the blame for French conservatism in literature on political circumstances. Out of fear of Napoleon, who strongly supported the old Neoclassical tradition once he became Emperor, dramatists were locked into a kind of stasis. The military cult of discipline was as evident in the strict rules in the theatre as in the rigid etiquette of the court. At last, however, the yoke had been thrown off, and literature too had won a new freedom, which Constant welcomes, though still with some reservations. He advocates for the French a modified form of the English and German liberty in the theatre, tempered always by reason. Twenty years after *Wallstein* Constant thus remains as circumspect and moderate as before. That he so openly admits his earlier mistakes reveals his innate honesty, and, above all, the extent of the advance in literary opinion during those intervening years.

That advance is plainly evident in Constant's *Réflexions sur la tragédie* which appeared in the same year as the second version of the *Wallstein* preface. In this treatise Constant makes fundamental distinctions between three types of tragedy. The first is tragedy of passion, such as *Phèdre* and *Andromaque*; this allows the observance of the three unities since passion acts swiftly. The second is tragedy of character, exemplified by *Hamlet*, *Egmont* and *Wallenstein*; this is less compatible with adherence to the unities because this type of tragedy requires time and latitude for its unfolding. And thirdly there is tragedy based on the action of society ('l'action de la société'); this Constant regards as the drama of the present and the future, believing that social forces and pressures represent a modern counterpart to the fatality of the ancients. It is to the delineation of this new mode of tragedy that Constant devotes the larger part of his *Réflexions sur la tragédie*. As it takes society for its starting-point, this new 'social tragedy' must give an extensive picture of the protagonists' environment, both physical and personal. Consequently, because of its broad canvas, it must relinquish the unities of time and place. ('En prenant l'action de la société sur l'homme pour ressort principal, la tragédie doit renoncer aux unités de temps et de lieu.'[40]) This third type of tragedy clearly refers to contemporary Romantic drama, for which Constant here offers a rationale. Though still prudent, and far from favouring any irrevocable break with the past, Constant is far more forward-looking and outspoken in his *Réflexions sur la tragédie* than in any of his earlier works. 'La révolution théâtrale s'opère'[41] ('the revolution in the theatre is under way'), he proclaims; 'la révolution littéraire est donc décidée; elle s'accomplit'[42] ('the literary revolution has been decided; it is taking place'); 'donnez la liberté, le génie mûrira'[43] ('grant freedom, genius will ripen'). These phrases show the profound change in the climate of French literary opinion between 1809 and 1829, a change to which Constant had himself in some measure contributed and which he now in turn reflects. Hugo's *Préface de 'Cromwell'* had appeared two years previously, and the *Réflexions sur la tragédie* themselves were written on the eve of the notorious performance of *Hernani*.

★   ★   ★   ★   ★

'Malgré leur politesse, mes observations ont laissé des traces'[44] ('in spite of their courteousness, my comments had some effect'), Constant wrote in 1829 of his *Quelques réflexions sur le théâtre allemand*. His pride is justified, for his preface to *Wallstein* was indeed a landmark in the evolution of French dramatic theory. Ironically, the play itself, in which Constant took so much pleasure at the time of composition, was soon relegated to the background; conversely, the preface that he added with reluctance was to have a lasting influence. And there is a further irony in the fact that against his will Constant was truly an innovator, though the term must be applied to him without any of the pejorative overtones with which he endowed it in his own mind.

Constant's preface to *Wallstein* was innovative in its clear and sympathetic delineation of an alternative approach to drama to the French Neoclassical canons. Those canons had been under criticism through much of the later eighteenth century; various amendments had been proposed to relax the rigidity in which the rules had become fixed. Constant was therefore not without antecedents.[45] Beaumarchais had pleaded for a revision of dramatic practices in his 1767 *Essai sur le genre dramatique sérieux*. But the most important of Constant's predecessors was, of course, Diderot, to whom he openly acknowledges his indebtedness by beginning his *Réflexions sur la tragédie* with a quotation from Diderot's *Entretiens sur Le Fils Naturel*.[46] Constant voices some disappointment at Diderot's failure to develop his ideas about 'social tragedy'. Diderot was in fact more concerned with the elaboration of what he called 'le genre sérieux'[47] and 'la tragédie domestique et bourgeoise'[48] modelled, like Lessing's *bürgerliches Trauerspiel*, on such English examples as Lillo's *The London Merchant*. Above all, Diderot was interested in the presence of realism in theatrical performance, in the physical mime of the actors. Mercier too, in his treatise *Du théâtre, ou Nouvel essai sur l'art dramatique* of 1773, pleaded for greater simplicity and realism, even for plainer language,[49] as well as for such concessions as the extension of the unity of time to sixty hours and that of place to three or four miles. But these were mere modifications of the existing system, whereas Constant brought a totally different kind of drama to the attention of the French. In this respect his role in France is a counterpart to that of Lessing who introduced Shakespeare to the Germans through his panegyrics in the *Literaturbriefe* (1759) and the *Hamburgische Dramaturgie* (1767). In both instances the discovery of a foreign model acted as a catalyst to the revitalisation of drama. And in a curious evolutionary chain, it was just those plays that were written in Germany under the impact of Shakespeare – the plays of Goethe and Schiller – that were destined to exert a similar stimulus in France through the intermediacy of Constant and Mme de Staël.

The true significance of Constant's preface thus emerges only when it is placed in its historical context. After the turmoil of the political Revolution had to some extent subsided, the *Réflexions sur le théâtre allemand* discreetly opened up the whole discussion of the current state of French drama in a debate that was to continue throughout the 1810s and 1820s until its frenzied climax in the so-called battle of *Hernani* at the end of that decade. Clearly, Constant was far ahead of his contemporaries – with the exception of Mme de Staël, whose judgements were, however, more haphazard than his. Beneath Constant's cautious formulations lies an enterprise of surprising boldness and imaginative insight. By implication at least he questions the very fundamentals of dramatic art as hitherto accepted in France through his confrontation with German practices. Constant's preface came to be regarded as the literary manifesto of a moderate liberalism which advocated a reasonable acceptance of foreign notions. With his exceptional powers of analysis, Constant was well able to discern those qualities of the German theatre that were lacking in the

French Neoclassical tradition: individuality in characterisation, freedom of expression in language and verse-form, and a certain breadth of horizon. These are the very features that were to become the hallmarks of French Romantic drama.

Constant's method, too, represented something of an innovation in France in its critical juxtaposition of contemporary cultures. In 1807, two years before Constant's preface, August Wilhelm Schlegel had measured Racine's *Phèdre* against the treatment of the same subject by Euripides, but that comparison was still largely reminiscent of the traditional confrontation between the ancients and the moderns. As for Charles de Villers' pamphlet of 1806, *De la manière essentiellement différente dont les poètes allemands et les français traitent l'amour*, it was a mere squib beside Constant's firework. Constant's approach plainly anticipates the comparative criticism of Mme de Staël's *De L'Allemagne* and of Stendhal's *Racine et Shakespeare*. In both matter and manner the preface to *Wallstein* was of vital importance for the subsequent evolution of dramatic criticism in France.

In this sense Constant, for all his caution and conservatism, was a precursor of the revolution in the French theatre. During a period of reaction, such as the Napoleonic Empire, when cosmopolitanism was suspect, his caution and conservatism were indeed cardinal virtues; and even after the fall of the Empire, when Neoclassicism had lost its official support, Constant's moderation remained an asset in an inflammatory situation, where susceptibilities were easily wounded. Always tactful and polite towards the native tradition, he took care to avow his attachment to French tragedy, declaring: 'La tragédie française est, selon moi, plus parfaite que celles des autres peuples'[50] ('French tragedy is, in my view, more perfect than that of other nations'). Far from belittling, let alone attacking, the native tradition, as did so many partisans of Romanticism, Constant seems, on the contrary, to be defending it. Through his skilful diplomacy he avoided the acerbity of those literary polemics in which the Romantic was envisaged as the opponent of the French. In fact the controversial word 'romantic' does not occur at all in Constant's writings on drama. The German Romantic element is presented not as a threat to the French theatre, but as a source of improvements which would further enhance the excellence of the native tradition. So Constant emerges as an adroit mediator, whose judiciousness persuades where virulence might well have antagonised.

NOTES TO CHAPTER 5

1. Benjamin Constant, *Journaux Intimes*, 30 August 1807, in *Oeuvres*, ed. Alfred Roulin (Paris: Gallimard, 1964) p. 624.
2. Harold G. Nicolson, *Benjamin Constant* (London: Constable, 1949) p. 184.
3. Benjamin Constant et Madame de Staël, *Lettres à un ami*, ed. Jean Mistler (Neuchâtel: La Baconnière, 1949) p. 93.
4. Victor Glachant, *Benjamiǹ Constant sous l'oeil du guet* (Paris: Plon, 1906) p. 118.
5. *Lettres de Benjamin Constant à sa famille, 1775–1830*, ed. Jean-H. Menos (Paris: Savine, 1888) p. 296.
6. E. Meyer, 'Benjamin Constant et *Wallstein*', *Prog. Gymn. zu Weimar*, 1898, pp. 17–21.
7. K. R. Gallas, 'La place du *Wallstein* de B. Constant dans l'évolution de la tragédie française', *Neophilologus*, xiii (1928), pp. 81–94.
8. Edmond Eggli, *Schiller et le romantisme français* (Paris: Gamber, 1927) vol. i, pp. 381–6.
9. Carlo Cordié, 'Il *Wallstein* di Benjamin Constant nelle testimonianze dell'autore e di alcuni suoi contemporanei', in *Studi in onore de Carlo Pellegrini*, ed. Glauco Natoli, Arnoldo Pizzorusso and Franco Simone (Torino: Societa editrice internazionale, 1963) pp. 411–54.
10. Benjamin Constant, *Wallstein*, ed. Jean-René Derré (Paris: Les Belles Lettres, 1965). All references to the text and the preface are to this edition.
11. Constant, *Wallstein*, p. 51.
12. Glachant, *Benjamin Constant sous l'oeil du guet*, p. 116.
13. Constant, *Oeuvres*, p. 909.
14. Constant, *Wallstein*, p. 50.
15. Glachant, *Benjamin Constant sous l'oeil du guet*, p. 117.
16. Constant, *Wallstein*, p. 57.
17. Jean-Louis Laya, in *Gazette nationale ou Le Moniteur universel*, xlvii (16 February 1809) 182.
18. Constant, *Wallstein*, p. 59.
19. Constant, *Wallstein*, pp. 61–2.
20. Constant, *Wallstein*, p. 62.
21. Schiller, *Wallensteins Tod*, act I, scene iv, and Constant, *Wallstein*, act III, scene i.
22. Jean-Louis Laya, in *Gazette nationale ou Le Moniteur universel*, lii (21 February 1809) 201.
23. Constant, *Oeuvres*, pp. 909–10.
24. Constant, *Wallstein*, pp. 65–7.
25. Constant, *Wallstein*, p. 96. I offer no translation of Constant's translation!
26. Constant, *Wallstein*, p. 51.
27. Constant, *Wallstein*, p. 52.
28. Madame de Staël, *De L'Allemagne*, ed. Jean de Pange and Simone Balayé

(Paris: Hachette, 1958) vol. ii, p. 317.

29. Glachant, *Benjamin Constant sous l'oeil du guet*, p. 125.
30. Constant, *Wallstein*, p. 52.
31. Constant, *Wallstein*, pp. 52–3.
32. Constant, *Wallstein*, p. 60.
33. 'Lettres de Benjamin Constant à Prosper de Barante, 1805–1830', *Revue des Deux Mondes*, xxxiv (15 July–1 August 1906) 250.
34. Constant. *Wallstein*, p. 56.
35. Constant. *Wallstein*, p. 60.
36. 'Lettres de Benjamin Constant à Prosper de Barante, 1805–1830', p. 269.
37. Constant, *Oeuvres*, p. 927.
38. Constant, *Oeuvres*, p. 865.
39. Constant, *Ouevres*, p. 881.
40. Constant, *Oeuvres*, p. 921.
41. Constant, *Oeuvres*, p. 927.
42. Constant, *Oeuvres*, p. 928.
43. Constant, *Oeuvres*, p. 928.
44. Constant, *Oeuvres*, p. 927.
45. Eggli, *Schiller et le romantisme français*, vol. i, pp. 381–6.
46. Denis Diderot, *Oeuvres*, ed. André Billy (Paris: Gallimard, 1951) p. 1257; Constant, *Oeuvres*, p. 901.
47. Diderot, *Oeuvres*, p. 1244.
48. Diderot, *Oeuvres*, p. 1232.
49. Louis-Sebastien Mercier, *Du théâtre, ou Nouvel essai sur l'art dramatique* (Amsterdam: Harrevelt, 1773) p. 301.
50. Constant, *Wallstein*, p. 67.

6 Two Versions of Schiller's *Wallenstein*

There can be few dramas as daunting to the prospective translator as Schiller's *Wallenstein*. The very qualities that constitute its greatness would surely be calculated to discourage the translator. The first obstacle is its inordinate size: *Wallenstein* comprises two full-length five-act plays, *Die Piccolomini* and *Wallensteins Tod*, as well as the eleven scenes of the prelude, *Wallensteins Lager*, so that a performance of the whole trilogy fills two entire evenings in the theatre. In keeping with its epic scope, its canvas is exceptionally broad; a complicated plot, intricate in its historical backcloth, is worked out in the interaction of a large number of psychologically differentiated figures. The language is as varied as the panorama, ranging from the robust colloquialisms of the common soldiers to the courtesies of the Imperial court and the tenderness of intimate family exchanges. At its centre stands Wallenstein, the source of the play's suspense and ultimately of its unending fascination. For he is a highly perplexing character, whose motives are never fully fathomed: in his parleying with the Swedes, is he betraying the Emperor, to whom he owes allegiance, or is he acting in the truest interests of his country by seeking to end the war? is he inspired by lust for personal power or by lofty idealism? is he in fact a traitor or a patriot? Schiller gives no definitive answer to such questions although as a professional historian (he had been appointed to the Chair of History at Jena in 1789) he devoted three years to a study of the Thirty Years' War, of which he published an account in 1793. It was, indeed, this historical research that gave rise to *Wallenstein* when Schiller, like the readers and spectators of his drama, fell increasingly under the spell of this provocative figure. The resultant trilogy is Schiller's greatest achievement, although its inherent complexities make it less readily accessible, even to native Germans, than *Maria Stuart* or *Wilhelm Tell*. Yet within ten years of its publication in 1800 two translations had appeared: the English version in 1800, within months of the German original, and the French one in 1809. Moreover, both were by men of distinction in their own right: Coleridge and Benjamin Constant. But starting from the same text and within a few years of each other, they produced utterly different translations. A comparison of their two versions reveals the curious factors that come into play in shaping not only a particular translation, but, beyond it, the whole process of literary transmission from one country to another.

In several respects the background to these two versions was remarkably similar. In both England and France the first wave of enthusiasm for Schiller and German drama was already declining by the turn of the century. As early as 1772 two volumes of German plays had appeared in a French translation by Junker and Liébault. They were followed by the more important *Nouveau théâtre allemand*, published by Friedel and Bonneville between 1782 and 1785. This collection of twenty-seven plays, including Goethe's *Götz von Berlichingen* and Schiller's *Die Räuber*, was – by one of those capricious twists of fortune so typical of foreign transmission – to exert greater influence in England than in France. For it was this French anthology of German plays that gave occasion to that momentous paper presented to the Royal Society of Edinburgh on 21 April 1788 by Henry Mackenzie, author of *The Man of Feeling*. This paper, subsequently printed in the *Edinburgh Magazine* of 1790 (xi, pp. 379–82) marks the first public mention of Schiller in Great Britain and also the virtual starting-point of the vogue for German drama. Undeterred by his apparent lack of German, Mackenzie reviewed a number of plays by Lessing and Goethe, but reserved his highest praise for Schiller's *Die Räuber*. His detailed account and startling panegyric aroused such widespread interest that there was a sudden spate of translations which took the literary world by storm.[1] Henceforth Schiller's fame in England was assured, and all his major plays to date were translated in the last decade of the eighteenth century: *Kabale und Liebe* in 1795, *Fiesco* in 1796, and *Don Carlos* in 1798. In England, as in France, Schiller's main appeal stemmed from his image as 'the untutored rebel against society',[2] the social dramatist, in short, the follower of Rousseau. The plays of his maturity, such as *Wallenstein*, were never to equal the success of his early Storm and Stress dramas, especially outside Germany. In France, for instance, Schiller was hardly known in the 1790s other than as the author of *Die Räuber*. Of this single play, however, at least three different versions were circulating under various titles: *Les Brigands* in the *Nouveau théâtre allemand*, Lamartelière's *Robert, Chef de brigands*, performed in 1792, and Creuzé de Lesser's *Les Voleurs* of 1795.

This intense early interest in Schiller waned in England and in France at about the same time, though not for the same reasons. In France it was political developments that halted the infiltration of German drama. During the *Directoire* and the *Consulat* there was a perceptible retreat from the liberties of the melodrama popular at the height of the Revolution. Under Napoleon's rule and with his personal support, the Neoclassical repertoire was restored to official favour as one of the glories of the French heritage. Napoleon himself was strongly attracted to the heroic ethos of Corneille, whose *Cinna* he is reputed to have seen no fewer than a dozen times.[3] This renewed pride in the native tradition fostered a distrust of foreign importations as dangerous novelties, a potential threat to the established French canon. It is certainly no coincidence that during this period of reaction in literary taste throughout the First Empire the number of translations from the German decreased quite abruptly. Nor is it an accident that Constant's *Wallstein* originated in a milieu notoriously hostile to the Emperor: Mme de Staël's circle at Coppet.

Coleridge's *Wallenstein*, too, ran counter to contemporary currents, for by 1800 the tide was well and truly turning against all things German. Paradoxically, the sudden recoil from German literature was a result of its inordinate success in England in the 1790s. Following the discovery of Bürger's ballad *Lenore* and of Kotzebue's melodramas, the enthusiasm for German literature had become a veritable mania: in one year alone there were no fewer than twenty-seven translations or adaptations from Kotzebue. Not surprisingly, these inferior importations, as they poured into the country, brought German writing into disrepute. Germany came to be regarded as the home of violent sensations, which were soon satirised in a series of parodies. In June 1798 already *The Anti-Jacobin* published *The Rovers, or the Double Arrangement* which, in spite of its title reminiscent of *The Robbers*, was directed not so much against Schiller as against Kotzebue. The butt of the attack was made plain in *The*

Benevolent Cut-Throat that appeared in 1800 in the periodical *The Meteors* and was attributed to a certain 'Klotzboggenhagen'. The British stage, Coleridge was to write later, was in urgent need of 'redemption . . . not only from horses, dogs, elephants, and the like zoological rarities, but also from the more pernicious barbarisms and Kotzebuisms in morals and taste', 'the speaking monsters imported from the banks of the Danube'.[4] So the early indiscriminate zeal cast discredit over German literature as a whole, and for a while even impeded serious study because no one wished to become associated with so infamous a topic. These circumstances account for the defensive tone of the letter Coleridge sent to the editor of the *Monthly Review* on 18 November 1800. It is worth quoting in full for the light it indirectly sheds on the repute of German drama in England at the time:

> In the review of my translation of Schiller's *Wallenstein* I am numbered among the Partizans of the German Theatre. As I am confident there is no passage in my Preface or Notes from which such an opinion can be legitimately formed: and, as the truth would not have been exceeded, if the directly contrary had been affirmed, I claim it of your justice that in your answers to Correspondents you would remove this misrepresentation. The mere circumstance of translating a manuscript play is not even evidence that I admired that one play, much less that I am a general admirer of the plays in the language.[5]

These words also foreshadow the attitude of Constant who was as anxious as Coleridge, though mainly for political reasons, not to be considered too ardent an advocate of German drama. It is a telling reflection of a strange historical situation that both translators were so eager to underline their critical detachment from the play they were translating, or rather from what it had come to represent.

There are further similarities in the genesis of the two translations. For neither Constant nor Coleridge came to the project entirely of his own volition. Constant seems to have had little acquaintance with Schiller before Mme de Staël suggested this scheme of translation to him in 1807. However, contrary to his own expectations, Constant soon warmed to his work and became increasingly absorbed in the problems of adaptation into

French, and eventually in the wider topic of German drama as a whole. These new interests which evolved out of the translation were to lead to the *Quelques réflexions sur le théâtre allemand* that were to prove of vital importance for the development of French Romantic drama.

Coleridge also underwent a change of heart in the course of his work on *Wallenstein*, but it was in the opposite direction to that of Constant. Coleridge's youthful attraction to Schiller is well known; he himself tells the dramatic tale of his reading of *The Robbers* in November 1794 in a note before his sonnet of 1796 'To the Author of *The Robbers*':

> One night in winter, leaving a College friend's room, with whom I had supped, I carelessly took away with me *The Robbers*, a drama, the very name of which I had never before heard of: – A winter midnight – the wind high – and *The Robbers* for the first time! The readers of Schiller will conceive what I felt. Schiller introduces no supernatural beings, yet his human beings agitate and astonish more than all the *goblin* rout – even of Shakespeare.

That same night, fresh still from the first impact, he wrote to ask Southey: 'who is this Schiller, this convulser of the heart? I tremble like an aspen leaf. Upon my soul, I write to you because I am frightened . . . Why have we ever called Milton sublime?'[6] With characteristic fervour Coleridge was soon planning to translate Schiller – in order thereby to defray the expenses of a journey to Jena! By the time he did go to Germany with Wordsworth in 1798–9 his early ardour seems already to have abated somewhat. He never actually met Schiller. Perhaps he was discouraged by his first personal contact with a German poet; judging by the account in *Biographia Literaria* (vol. ii, pp. 169–80), his interview with Klopstock can hardly have been a pleasure, conducted as it was partly in French interpreted by Wordsworth, and partly in Latin barely comprehensible to either side because of the differences between the English and the Continental pronounciation. It was after his return from Germany, late in 1799, that Coleridge was commissioned to translate *Wallenstein*. The vogue for things German was still sufficiently strong to warrant such a venture, with little sign as yet of the sharp decline that was to come the following year. This translation of *Wallenstein* was a commercial transaction of a bizarre nature. Schiller himself sold a manuscript copy (for less than £60 incidentally) to the bookseller Bell, the leading English dealer in German drama. From Bell it passed to the publisher Longman and thence back to Coleridge who was asked to translate it with the utmost speed. His version was completed in six weeks (about the same time it took Constant) so as to appear simultaneously with the German original. The pressure of the short deadline may have contributed to Coleridge's acute disenchantment, voiced in several letters, in which he complains that the work 'wasted and depressed my spirits, and left a sense of wearisomeness and disgust'.[7] The translation of *Wallenstein* was, in fact, the *coup de grâce* to Coleridge's interest in Schiller, whereas it was the starting-point of Constant's.

★   ★   ★   ★   ★

The textual divergences between the English and the French versions are as far-reaching as their subtitles imply. Coleridge plainly states that his are dramas 'translated from the German of Schiller'; Constant, on the other hand, simply calls his *Wallstein* a 'tragédie en cinq actes et en vers' without so much as a mention of Schiller's name on the title-page. This aptly reflects the contrast between the two renderings: the English is a close translation of the German, while the French is a free adaptation. In their respective choice of format, both Coleridge and Constant were conforming to the established practices of their own lands in more than one sense. In England in the ten years preceding Coleridge's *Wallenstein* it had become standard usage to market straight translations of German drama.[8] France, on the other hand, preferred the adaptation as shown by the multiple versions of *Die Räuber*. Translation, adaptation, imitation: these were for long terms so fluid and flexible that it is often not easy to distinguish between a play translated directly from another language and one more remotely based on a foreign model. Schiller's dramas were favourite sources of inspiration, particularly *Die Jungfrau von Orleans* which prompted innumerable French works about Joan of Arc; *Maria Stuart* was also popular, even turning up as a melodramatic musical in Duperche's *Alix et Blanche ou Les illustres rivales* of 1813. This licence – not to say, unscrupulousness – in the exploitation of models makes it extraordinarily difficult to assess with any degree of accuracy the true position of Schiller (and indeed Shakespeare) in France – notwithstanding Edmond Eggli's informative volumes on *Schiller et le romantisme français* (Paris: Gamber, 1927). Constant's method of fashioning a thoroughly French play from a foreign paradigm was as customary in France as was Coleridge's straightforward translation in England.

In yet another and much more significant way Coleridge and Constant were affected by the dominant literary traditions of their native countries. In transferring *Wallenstein* into their own idiom, they faced entirely different problems because the dramatic conventions of the two literatures were so utterly disparate. To the Frenchman of the early nineteenth century serious tragedy still meant primarily the plays of Racine and Corneille: harmonious in form and expression, finite in their outward appearance but infinite in their exploration of human passions. The Shakespearean chronical play is almost the opposite pole to French analytical drama: far freer in form and language, more open in construction, and highly individualistic in its imaginative range. It was largely because they were transposing *Wallenstein* onto such heterogeneous backgrounds that Coleridge and Constant produced such widely differing versions, for both, to a large extent, assimilated the German original to the indigenous modes.

This process of naturalisation into the home culture is much more striking in Constant's case than in Coleridge's. The reason is simple: Schiller's *Wallenstein* is closer to the English Shakespearean dramatic mould than to the French Neoclassical pattern. Consequently, Constant had to make more fundamental modifications to the German play than Coleridge in order to achieve a degree of adaptation sufficient to make his version acceptable to his compatriots. Indeed, the changes that he imposed are so radical that they almost justify the omission of Schiller's name from the title-page.

Of the many alterations that Constant made only one also occurs in the English version: Coleridge, too, suppressed *Wallensteins Lager*. His motives for so doing are not at all clear. In the *Preface of the Translator to the First Edition* he writes that 'it would have been unadvisable from the incongruity of those lax verses with the present taste of the English Public'.[9] Cryptic though this statement is, it does suggest that the loosely structured fragment of local colour struck Coleridge as too amorphous even for the English stage. He failed to grasp the function of the *Lager* in the economy of the whole trilogy, or else he would not have maintained that 'Schiller's intention seems to have been merely to have prepared his readers for the Tragedies by a lively picture of the laxity of discipline, and the mutinous dispositions of Wallenstein's soldiery'.[10] Certainly the prelude prepares the reader or spectator, but not just by its portrayal of the soldiers' mutinous dispositions; its real significance lies in its indirect revelation of Wallenstein's charismatic power through the spell he casts over the whole camp. Had Coleridge realised this, he would not so readily have concluded that 'it is not necessary as a preliminary explanation. For these reasons it has been thought expedient not to translate it'[11] Having thus disposed of the *Lager*, Coleridge re-grouped the rest of the material so as to have two plays of approximately equal length. (In the German, *Die Piccolomini* is appreciably shorter than *Wallensteins Tod* because it is usually performed together with the *Lager*.) Hence *The Piccolomini* comprises the German play of that name plus the first two acts of *Wallensteins Tod*, while *The Death of Wallenstein* consists of the last three, extremely long acts of *Wallensteins Tod*.

Apart from this re-arrangement Coleridge altered remarkably little. A close comparison of the English text with the German original is, regrettably, not possible because Coleridge was translating from a handwritten manuscript which is no longer available. There are some departures from the printed German text: whether these are attributable to the whim of the translator cannot be determined. Nor can one check Derwent Coleridge's contention that 'about 250 lines were omitted, and there are some additions and substitutions'.[12] However, there is comical evidence of the illegibility of the German manuscript, although Coleridge had had it specially copied into Roman (from Gothic) script so as to facilitate its sale in England. Only misreading can account for such strange distortions as 'Glogan' for 'Glogau',[13] 'Fachau' for 'Tachau',[14] 'Tirschenseil' for 'Tirschenreit',[15] and the proper name 'Gordon' as a rendering of 'Garden'[16] meaning 'guards'! This latter misreading raises the problem of Coleridge's fairly numerous linguistic errors, which have been the object of more attention than any other feature of his translation.[17] That Coleridge was uncertain of his German is apparent from one of his footnotes: 'fearful of having made some blunder, I add the

original'.[18] In fact he made a good many startling blunders, many
of which clearly stem from an inadequate comprehension of
idiomatic German. There are conflicting reports concerning his
proficiency in the language. He was undoubtedly learning – and
translating from – it as early as 1796, and during his stay in
Germany he extended his studies to Old High German and
Gothic; he purported to be writing poetry in German and to be
reading it as fluently as English. On the other hand, he never
seems to have been able to speak it, and his friends in Germany
were by no means as confident of his competence as he was. Nor
was Coleridge in a position, during his hurried translation, to
consult a native German as easily as Constant could in the
multilingual community at Coppet. His version does raise the
question as to his capacity later to cope with Kant, Schelling and
Fichte, by no means the easiest of German.

In spite of the linguistic errors, Coleridge's translation is
highly faithful to the original. He himself set great store by
fidelity: 'I endeavoured to render my Author literally',[19] he states
in the *Preface*, and at several points he inserted a footnote
avowing that a certain phrase 'might have been rendered with
more literal fidelity',[20] or excusing what seemed to him an
excessive liberty. In the face of these repeated apologies, it is
perhaps ironical to criticise the English text on the grounds that it
is at times *too* close to the German. Coleridge made such a fetish
of literalness that his English appears stilted and uncouth, specially towards the beginning. It becomes livelier as soon as he
ventures to depart from the original by adding imagery or
turning abstractions into more concrete terms. His version is,
indeed, most successful in those very places where he considers it
a failure: 'I found it not in my power to translate this song with
literal fidelity'.[21] he confesses of his rendering of Thekla's song.
Deficient though it may be in '*literal* fidelity', it does have real
poetic beauty.

★   ★   ★   ★   ★

These two versions of *Wallenstein* illustrate two alternative approaches to the problem of transposing a work of art from one
language into another: either direct, more or less literal translation, or an attempt at an artistic re-creation. The method selected
is usually determined, in part at least, by the intermediary's own

predilections. Generally, the stronger the translator's innate creative urge, the further will he depart from the original towards an independent production. An outstanding example of such free re-working occurs in Stefan George's rendering of Baudelaire's *Fleurs du mal*; a poet with a style so personal as to be idiosyncratic, George assimilated Baudelaire's poems to his own manner to such an extent that he aptly characterised the resultant translations as 'umdichtungen'[22] (literally: 'transpoetisations'). In the case of Coleridge and Constant, neither was an inventive dramatist in his own right. The decisive factor in the choice of format was, therefore, not personal preference, but rather the demands of the idiom and traditions into which Schiller's play was being introduced. At that particular point in literary history outer forces exerted considerable pressures on the intermediary, especially in France, where dramatic form was for many years a prime bone of contention in the emergence of the Romantic movement. So it was that Constant, given the circumstances of his time, had to change *Wallenstein* radically if it was to stand any hope of acceptance by the French. Even so, in spite of all his efforts to adjust Schiller's trilogy to native tastes, his *Wallstein* proved unpalatable to his compatriots. Coleridge, by contrast, had no need of such tactics of acclimatisation because of the distinct similarities between English and German drama at that period. Shakespeare was in fact the inspiration of the *Sturm und Drang* dramatists, including the young Schiller. Coleridge was aware of the affinity, for he suggests in the *Preface* that 'we should proceed to the perusal of Wallenstein, not from Lear or Othello, but from Richard the Second, or the three parts of Henry the Sixth'.[23] Coleridge even follows Shakespearean practice in casting the speech of servants and soldiers into prose. Thus he too assimilated the German play to native tradition, although this involved none of the drastic reorganisation that Constant had to undertake.

The ultimate fate of these two translations of *Wallenstein* is unlike, except that it was not, in either case, directly related to their intrinsic quality. Coleridge was patently unfortunate in the timing of his version, in its coincidence with the abrupt decrease of public interest in German matters. For instance, *The German Muse*, a periodical devoted to German affairs, founded in January 1800, had to cease publication in June 1801, after only three issues, for lack of readers. This would seem to suggest that the revulsion against the German theatre was as sudden and violent as the earlier upsurge of enthusiasm. Under these circumstances it is hardly surprising that Coleridge's *Wallenstein* found neither a favourable critical reception nor a ready sale. At best it was rather grudgingly conceded that 'the pieces are more regular than many other productions of the German theatre; and they are at least free from absurdity', but the same anonymous critic deemed the translation 'languid' and the plot 'insufferably tedious'.[24] Only Scott seems to have been impressed by it, for he derived from *Wallenstein* mottoes for the chapter headings of his *Waverley* novels. In fact, Coleridge himself was the first to detract from *Wallenstein* when he introduced the play with the comment:

> The admirers of Schiller, who have abstracted their concep-
> tion of that author from the *Robbers* and *Cabal and Love*, plays
> in which the main interest is produced by the excitement of
> curiosity and in which the curiosity is excited by terrible and
> extraordinary incident, will not have perused without some
> portion of disappointment the dramas which it has been my
> employment to translate.[25]

This remark is symptomatic of Coleridge's estrangement from Schiller and from German drama. The drudgery of translating *Wallenstein* marked a turning-point in his attitude to Schiller. His judgements became increasingly adverse with the passage of time. In October 1800, six months after completing the work, Coleridge wrote: 'I would not stir 20 yards out of my way to know him'[26] (Schiller). This emotionalistic rejection later gave way to more substantial criticisms: 'Schiller has the material Sublime; to produce an effect, he sets you a whole town on fire, and throws infants with their mothers into the flames, or locks up a father in an old tower. But Shakespeare drops a handker-chief, and the same or greater effects follow.'[27] That was written in 1822; by 1834 he had grown still harsher: 'Schiller's blank verse is bad. He moves in it as a fly in a glue bottle. His thoughts have their connection and variety, it is true, but there is no sufficiently corresponding movement in the verse. How differ-ent from Shakespeare's endless rhythms!'[28] This repeated ten-dency to size Schiller up against Shakespeare, as he had already done in his first excited response in the prefatory note to 'The Author of *The Robbers*', is of crucial importance for an understanding of Coleridge's – and indeed the British – change of attitude towards Schiller. Flattering though the comparison was to Schiller at the outset, in the long run it proved to his disadvantage. For once Schiller had developed beyond the rebelliousness of his early *Sturm und Drang* plays, he merely seemed like an echo of Shakespeare. And the English, with their Shakespearean heritage, had no need to import dramas such as *Wallenstein*. The flow of dramatic trade was predominantly in the other direction as the impetus from England sparked the revival in Europe. Shakespeare was the vital force that inspired Goethe and Schiller as well as Hugo and Dumas. Yet at the same time their English contemporaries, Shelley and Byron, favoured a markedly lyrical type of drama. Perhaps this too contributed to the lack of artistic or intellectual response to *Wallenstein* in England.

Yet, curiously, from the commercial point of view, it reaped lasting success, for this translation by Coleridge went on to become the standard version throughout the nineteenth century on both sides of the Atlantic. It was first published in London by Pickering in 1828. Then it was reprinted separately in London in 1840 by Moxon, and in 1842 by Smith before being included in Bohn's Standard Library in 1846, in the Universal Library (Ingram & Cooke) in 1853, and in the Masterpieces of Foreign Literature (Griffin) in 1866. *Wallensteins Lager* had been translated by John Churchill in 1831 (in *Fraser's Magazine for Town and Country*, ii, 127–52) and was included with Coleridge's rendering of *Die Piccolomini* and *Wallensteins Tod* in these later collections. In the United States, Coleridge's *The Piccolomini* was printed in New York by Longworth in 1805. The complete trilogy did not come until much later in the century, and then in a succession of editions of Schiller's works: in 1861 in Philadelphia (Kohler), again in Philadelphia in 1883 though with a different publisher (Barrie), the following year in New York (Williams) in a so-called 'Household Edition', in 1902 in Boston (Nicolls) and in 1915 in New York in the German Publishing Society's series German Classics of the Nineteenth and Twentieth Centuries. These are just the major editions on both sides of the Atlantic; many of them were reprinted at frequent intervals.[29]

By contrast, the French *Wallstein* was a sensation, if not exactly a success. The literary journals of the day gave lengthy accounts of the piece, which provoked heated arguments. It was branded a literary monstrosity ('une monstruosité littéraire') by

the *Journal de Paris* of 12 February 1809. On the French scene it
appeared not only as potentially threatening to the native dramatic tradition, but also as politically suspect in its tale of defection
from an emperor. For these reasons, on the advice of Mme de
Staël, Constant prefaced the published text with *Quelques réflexions sur le théâtre allemand*. Though added as an afterthought,
largely in self-defence, the *Réflexions* are very much longer and
wider in scope than Coleridge's cursory *Preface of the Translator*.
Since Constant's discourse was conceived primarily as an
apologia, he begins with a consideration of the problems attendant on rendering Schiller's trilogy into French: the enormous
length of the whole work, the unfamiliarity of the subject-
matter, Thekla's lack of decorum, Wallenstein's superstititions,
and above all, the freedom of expression and the realism customary in the German theatre. From this frank and illuminating
discussion of his own difficulties, Constant is drawn – possibly
against his initial intentions – to an outline comparison of the
German and the French approaches in drama: the German is
broader in scope, more complex in characterisation, and freer,
i.e. more direct and realistic in mode and speech than French
tragedy with its formalistic emphasis on smoothness and simplicity. In this analysis of the fundamental differences between the
two types of drama Constant reveals intellectual acuity and a
sensitive insight into the distinctive qualities of Schiller's plays.
This true appreciation is curiously lacking in Coleridge in spite of
his long-standing enthusiasm for Schiller and his sojourn in
Germany. Constant's deeper comprehension of Schiller helps to
explain a paradox that at first sight seems baffling: the English
version, which is the better of the two, judged purely as a
translation, proved of less artistic significance in the long run
than the undeniably feeble French adaptation. For while *Wallstein* itself was soon forgotten and superseded in the theatre by
the more effective rendering of Charles Liadières, the *Quelques
réflexions sur le théâtre allemand* that arose out of Constant's
encounter with German drama were of far-reaching importance
for the evolution of French drama. Here, for the first time, the
French were presented with an intelligent appraisal of the German theatre. What is more, Constant showed exemplary tact and
caution in his inferences. Though conscious of the virtues of
German drama, he categorically states: 'Je suis loin de recommander l'introduction de ces moyens dans nos tragédies'[30] ('I am

far from recommending the introduction of these methods into our tragedies'); for, whatever its defects, 'la tragédie française est, selon moi, plus parfaite que celle des autres peuples'[31] ('French tragedy is, in my view, more perfect than that of other peoples'). Thanks to his astuteness, Constant was thus able to dispel some of the instinctive French fears of foreign importations; far from displacing the native mode, German drama was further to enrich it. In this way the *Quelques réflexions sur le théâtre allemand* adroitly fostered the dramatic renewal in France.

What then is the outcome of this strange episode of the two versions of *Wallenstein*? First, it should serve as a reminder of the peculiar waywardness of international literary transmissions. The process is far from rational, governed as it is to a considerable extent by factors as capricious as changing public taste, national prejudices and phobias. Over and beyond this general lesson, however, a more specific conclusion can be drawn that is of immediate relevance to an understanding of European Romanticism. It is the relativity of the historical sense of the term 'romantic'. In this episode of *Wallenstein* and its English and French translations, we see a play perceived in quite a different manner in the three countries at the same time. To the Germans of the opening years of the nineteenth century *Wallenstein* represented the zenith of their Classical theatre. To the French, who viewed it against the background of their own Neoclassical tradition, it seemed the incarnation of a dangerous licentiousness. And for the English with their Shakespearean heritage it simply lacked the interest of novelty. So this play, that holds pride of place in its own national literature, was too avante-garde for one of its neighbours, and simultaneously too passé for the other. This is surely a striking illustration of the diversity of viewpoint in the three countries within a single decade. Even at the height of the Romantic movement there was patently no unanimity of opinion as to what was 'romantic'.

NOTES TO CHAPTER 6

1. L. A. Willoughby, 'English Translations and Adaptations of Schiller's *Robbers*', *Modern Language Review*, xvi (July–Oct. 1921) 297–315.
2. L. A. Willoughby, 'Schiller in England and Germany', *Publications of the English Goethe Society*, xi (1935) p. 1.
3. See Frederick G. Healey, *The Literary Culture of Napoleon* (Geneva: Droz,

and Paris: Minard 1959). Appendix B (p. 156) lists the plays Napoleon saw and the number of performances of each at which he was present.

4. Samuel Taylor Coleridge, *Biographia Literaria*, ed. J. Shawcross, rev. ed. (London: Oxford University Press, 1958) vol. ii, p. 181.
5. Coleridge, letter to *Monthly Review*, xxxiii (1800) 336.
6. Coleridge, *Letters*, ed. Ernest Hartley Coleridge (London: Heinemann, 1895) vol. i, pp. 96–7.
7. Coleridge, *Biographia Epistolaris*, ed. A. Turnbull (London: Bell, 1911) p. 193.
8. See F. W. Stokoe, *German Influence in the English Romantic Period* (Cambridge: Cambridge Univ. Press, 1926) Appendix V, pp. 180–7.
9. Coleridge, *Complete Poetical Works*, ed. Ernest Hartley Coleridge (Oxford: Clarendon Press, 1912) vol. ii, p. 724. All subsequent references are to this edition.
10. Coleridge, *Complete Poetical Works*, vol. ii, p. 724.
11. Coleridge, *Complete Poetical Works*, vol. ii, p. 724.
12. Preface to Coleridge's *Dramatic Works* (London: Moxon, 1852) p. xii.
13. *Death of Wallenstein*, act III, scene iii, and *Wallensteins Tod*, act IV, scene iii.
14. *Death of Wallenstein*, act III, scene iv, and *Wallensteins Tod*, act IV, scene iv.
15. *Death of Wallenstein*, act III, scene iv, and *Wallensteins Tod*, act IV, scene ii.
16. *Death of Wallenstein*, act IV, scene ii, and *Wallensteins Tod*, act V, scene ii.
17. The errors were first listed in *The Westminster Review*, July 1850 (reprinted in Derwent Coleridge's edition of Coleridge's *Dramatic Works* (London: Moxon, 1852) pp. 426–7). P. Machule's article, 'Coleridges Wallenstein-übersetzung', *Englische Studien*, xxxi (1902) 182–239, consists almost exclusively of an enumeration of errors, pedantic and at times itself mistaken.
18. Coleridge, *Complete Poetical Works*, vol. ii, p. 644.
19. Coleridge, *Complete Poetical Works*, vol. ii, p. 599.
20. Coleridge, *Complete Poetical Works*, vol. ii, p. 701.
21. Coleridge, *Complete Poetical Works*, vol. ii, p. 653. Italics are Coleridge's.
22. See Lilian R. Furst, 'Stefan George's *Die Blumen des Bösen*: A Problem of Translation', *Revue de littérature comparée*, xlviii, No. 2 (1974) 203–17.
23. Coleridge, *Complete Poetical Works*, vol. ii, p. 725.
24. *Monthly Review*, xxxiii (1800) 128.
25. Coleridge, *Complete Poetical Works*, vol. ii, p. 724.
26. *Letters from the Lake Poets to Daniel Stuart, 1800–1838* (Privately printed, 1889) p. 15, letter viii, from Coleridge, Greta Hall, Keswick, 7 October 1800.
27. Coleridge, *Table Talk*, 29 December 1822.
28. Coleridge, *Table Talk*, 2 June 1834.
29. See *Schiller in England, 1787–1960*, a bibliography compiled under the direction of Robert Pick. *Publications of the English Goethe Society*, xxx (1961).
30. Benjamin Constant, *Wallstein*, ed. Jean-René Derré (Paris: Les Belles Lettres, 1965) p. 56.
31. Constant, *Wallstein*, p. 67.

7 Novalis' *Hymnen an die Nacht* and Nerval's *Aurélia*

The adjective 'incomparable' is given two meanings in the Oxford English Dictionary: 'not to be, not capable of being, compared' and 'without equal; peerless, matchless, unique'. The word has frequently been applied in both its connotations to Novalis' *Hymnen an die Nacht* and also – quite independently, it should be noted – to Gérard de Nerval's *Aurélia*.

The *Hymnen* have been called 'einzigartig'[1] ('unique'), 'ohnegleichen'[2] ('without parallel'), 'originell und einsam'[3] ('original and isolated'). Their exceptional place in the history of German literature has repeatedly been emphasised by every major critic since Rudolf Haym: 'Er dichtete die *Hymnen an die Nacht*, jene tiefsinnig schwermuthsvollen Laute klagender Verzückung und inbrünstigen Schmerzes, mit nichts zu vergleichen, was unsre klassische Poesie hervorgebracht hat, mit nichts auch, was wir bisher von der nachgoethischen, der romantischen Poesie kennen gelernt haben.'[4] ('He composed the *Hymns to the Night*, those profoundly melancholy cadences of anguished ecstasy and passionate grief, comparable to nothing either in our classical poetry or indeed in post-Goethean romantic poetry.') The same idea was elaborated fifty years later by Paul Kluckhohn, who stressed the uniqueness of the *Hymnen* in the framework both of German literature and of Novalis' works in contrast to the more traditionalistic *Geistlichen Lieder*: 'Haben die *Hymnen an die Nacht* in der deutschen Dichtung eine ganz isolierte Stellung, hervorgegangen aus einem ganz persönlichen Erleben einer differenzierten Einzelpersönlichkeit, so reihen sich die *Geistlichen Lieder* in den Entwicklungsgang des Gemeindegesanges ein, stehen in einer Tradition.'[5] ('While the *Hymns to the Night* stand in a totally isolated position in German literature as the uniquely personal experience of a singular individual, the

Spiritual Songs, on the other hand, are integrated into the development of the communal hymn and form part of a tradition.') More recently, H. A. Korff made the identical point when he described the *Hymnen* as 'eine Poesie die in der Geschichte unserer Dichtung einzig ist'[6] ('a poetic work unique in the history of our literature').

The judgements passed on Nerval's *Aurélia* are remarkably like those on the *Hymnen*; indeed, but for the language and the national frame of reference, they are virtually interchangeable. All the phrases just cited about the *Hymnen* are equally pertinent to *Aurélia*. Conversely, comments on *Aurélia*, even while insisting on that work's incomparability, are strangely apposite to the *Hymnen*: 'cet étrange travail, sans exemple'[7] ('this strange, unprecedented work'); 'cette oeuvre, à laquelle on ne peut en comparer aucune autre'[8] ('this work that is comparable to no other'); 'most intensely personal, . . . unique';[9] 'the most marvellous specimen of dream literature in French';[10] 'unique for its literary, or simply human merits';[11] 'ein eigenes Werk'[12] ('a singular work'). Albert Béguin's words are in fact an exact counterpart to those of Korff: 'une poésie qui est sans exemple dans l'histoire des lettres françaises'[13] ('a poetic work unprecedented in the history of French literature'). And the conclusions of Aristide Marie, too, are as valid for the *Hymnen* as for *Aurélia*:

> Que dire encore de ces pages, dont on chercherait vainement ailleurs l'accent d'outre-terre? Car nul écrivain, même entre les adeptes de l'occulte et les évocateurs de l'invisible, n'est apte à produire pareille intensité d'émotion. Ni les *Mémorables* de Swedenborg, ni les rêves opiacés de Quincey, ni les sataniques figures d'Hoffmann, ni les macabres évocations de Poe ne nous éloignent du réel à ce degré.[14]

> (What more is one to say of these pages, whose transcendental tones would be sought in vain elsewhere? For no writer, not even among the votaries of the occult and the diviners of the unseen, is capable of such intensity of feeling. Not Swedenborg's *Memorials* nor de Quincey's opium dreams, nor Hoffmann's satanic figures, nor Poe's macabre imaginings remove us thus far from reality.)

That Marie did not mention Novalis' *Hymnen* is surprising, for they are far more akin to *Aurélia* in content, spirit and form than the works that he adduces. Incomparable though the *Hymnen* and *Aurélia* may be in one sense of the word, they are nonetheless very clearly comparable to each other.

Both works are deeply subjective, and subjective in a manner and to a degree startling in their respective countries at their time of publication. In Germany at the turn of the nineteenth century and in France towards the middle of that century there was, of course, no dearth of personal poetry; Goethe's early lyrics and the poetry of Lamartine are obvious examples of the spontaneous expression of intimate feelings prompted by personal experience. But the *Hymnen* and *Aurélia* are more radically subjective than this traditional lyricism, for which the outer world, specially the realm of nature, still remains objectively valid, even though coloured by the personal emotion of the beholder. The *Hymnen* and *Aurélia* are descended from this line of intimate poetry in that both have a personal source – even a curiously parallel source in the deaths of Sophie Kühn and Jenny Colon. So on one level these works are alike as chapters of inner autobiography, documents of a turning-point in the lives of their authors. Yet in both instances the personal experience is the occasion, rather than the subject matter.

The real theme of the *Hymnen* and of *Aurélia* is not grief at the loss of the beloved, but the fervid visions that are the poet's response to his situation. In both works it is these visions that are central to the structure and meaning, and that are therefore so much more vivid and immediate than the desolate, ordinary world. Novalis often uses terms of greyness and mistiness to describe reality: 'des ganzen langen Lebens kurze Freuden und vergebliche Hoffnungen kommen in grauen Kleidern wie Abendnebel nach der Sonne Untergang' ('the brief joys and vain hopes of one's whole long life come in grey garments like evening mists after sunset' – first *Hymn*). The sun has set on this world, leaving it extinguished ('verlöscht' – third *Hymn*), bleak, consumed ('verzehrt' – second *Hymn*) by despair. By contrast, the sun has risen on the other world, the world of night with its enthralling visions. The inner realm has all the attributes of light, joy and energy usually associated with life; it is 'erfreulich' ('joyous'), 'leuchtend' ('radiant'), 'blitzend' ('flashing'), 'kräftig' ('vigorous'), 'wach' ('awake' – first *Hymn*), illumined by the resplendent light of his visions that turn night and death into day and life. A line from the beginning of the second part of Novalis' *Heinrich von Ofterdingen*, 'Die Welt wird Traum, der Traum wird Welt' ('The world becomes a dream, the dream becomes a world') could serve as an epigraph to the *Hymnen*, and indeed to *Aurélia* too. For Nerval, as for Novalis, 'le Rêve est une seconde vie' ('the Dream is a second life'), to quote the opening phrase of *Aurélia*. The dreams of this second life are more exciting than his real life, filled as they are with wondrous creatures and dramatic happenings. They also have intrinsic worth for Nerval because of 'cette idée que je m'étais faite du rêve comme ouvrant à l'homme une communication avec le monde des esprits'[15] ('this notion I had evolved for myself of the dream as man's gateway to communication with the world of spirits'). Thus 'l'imagination m'apportait des délices infinies' ('imagination brought me infinite delights' – i, 359), adding a whole new dimension to his existence and eventually transforming it, as for Novalis. Such incursion of dream into reality is a common theme in Nerval's writings, recurring in many of his poems as well as in the *Histoire du Calife Hakim*, the *Roman tragique*, and most strikingly in the *Biographie singulière de Raoul Spifame* who 'avait le conviction que ses rêves étaient sa vie et que sa prison n'était qu'un rêve' ('was convinced that his dreams were his life and that his prison was merely a dream' – ii, 942). But nowhere is 'l'épanchement du songe dans la vie réelle' ('the effusion of dream into real life' – i, 363) as prominent as in *Aurélia*. Nerval seeks to 'forcer ces portes mystiques', 'chercher le sens de mes rêves' ('force these mystical doors', 'find out the meaning of my dreams' – i, 412) because he believes that the ultimate truth is revealed indirectly in the esoteric visions of his inner eye. Thus Nerval resembles Novalis in this attempt at a total re-assessment of life from the vantage point of a private revelation.

It is in this sense that the *Hymnen* and *Aurélia* go beyond the merely personal into the fundamentally subjective. Their subjectivism is that outlined in Fichte's *Wissenschaftslehre*, whereby the world is refashioned according to the perceptions of the individual imagination. For both Novalis and Nerval the imagination was the prime creative faculty, and the interior realm it conjured up was at least as real as, and much more vital than, the outer universe perceived by the senses. For this reason the *Hymnen* and *Aurélia* may be regarded as early – and superb – examples of 'a literature in which the visible world is no longer a reality, and the unseen world no longer a dream',[16] to use Arthur Symons' characterisation of Symbolism. In both works the mystical insights of the dream world lead to a revaluation of the hitherto accepted values, expanding outwards from the personal experience to the destiny of man in general. The beloved is transfigured into an interceding angel and associated with the Virgin Mary. Novalis, in the fifth *Hymn*, reviews the entire history of mankind, interpreting the advent of Christianity as a parallel to his own illumination. Nerval too looks back into the past and mythologises it. As Béguin has so admirably put it:

> La transfiguration de sa propre vie en un mythe comprenant tout le destin de ses semblables; la conscience toujours plus nette du lien qui existe entre la solution du drame métaphysique et la fin de ses tourments personnels; la nécessité de vaincre la menace de la mort par la conquête mystique de la lumière finale: telle est la valeur, triple et pourtant unique, que Nerval donne à sa tentative pour "diriger son rêve".[17]

> (The transfiguration of his own life into a myth embracing the whole destiny of his fellow-men; the increasingly clear awareness of the link between the resolution of the metaphysical conflict and the end of his personal torments; the need to overcome the threat of death by the mystical conquest of the ultimate illumination: that is the threefold yet single import of Nerval's attempt to "direct his dream".)

Béguin's summation of *Aurélia* brings out once more the parallelism with the *Hymnen* in that his words are as fitting to the one as to the other.

Analogous too is the direction in which Novalis and Nerval move: 'du sein du désespoir' ('from the depths of despair') towards 'les voies lumineuses de la religion' ('the luminescent paths of religion' – i, 412). Novalis follows the straighter route. From the prison of despair which he evokes towards the beginning of the first *Hymn* and again, even more sharply, in the opening lines of the third, he is released through the grace of his visions, which bring a new meaning to his existence and a new faith in the life-to-come. In the light of his central revelation he surveys his own past, present and future (in the second and fourth *Hymns*) in a kind of rebirth experience. This he extends to all mankind in the fifth *Hymn*, where he equates the role of Christ in history with that of the vision of Sophie in his own life. The strong religious colouring, in attitude as well as in language, is particularly evident in the latter three *Hymns*. At the beginning of the fourth already there are references to the cross, to pilgrimage, to the Promised Land; the fifth *Hymn* is in praise of Christianity in plainly Biblical phraseology, while the final one is a song of salvation, akin in tone and form to the *Geistlichen Lieder*:

> Hinunter zu der süssen Braut,
> Zu Jesus, Dem Geliebten –
> Getrost die Abenddämmrung graut
> Den Liebenden, Betrübten.
> Ein Traum bricht unsre Banden los
> Und senkt uns in des Vaters Schoss.

> (Towards the sweet bride,
> To Jesus, the Beloved –
> The grey dusk of evening sinks with comfort
> On lovers, on the sorrowing.
> A dream breaks our bonds
> And delivers us into our Father's keeping.)

With these closing words of the *Hymnen* Novalis has assuredly turned into the luminescent paths of religion.

Nerval's progress is complicated by a psychological factor absent in Novalis: a sense of guilt. Following the death of Aurélia, Nerval is beset by a dual consciousness of grief: sorrow at the loss of his beloved, and panic at his loss of God, that is associated in his mind with her death, for which he feels responsible through his unworthiness. The resultant sense of guilt emerges clearly in his repeated plaints of 'ma condamnation' ('my doom' – i, 389) and his 'remords les plus graves' ('deepest remorse' – i, 392), culminating in his fear that 'je suis perdu' ('I am lost' – i, 398). In these expressions of despair Nerval often uses words of a religious hue; *Aurélia*, like the *Hymnen*, abounds in Biblical references to the apostles, to Noah and the flood, to Jacob's fight with the angel, to stories of temptation. That Nerval should recall from the Bible stories of struggle is significant because he himself has to fight for that salvation which is bestowed on Novalis by grace. When Nerval finally achieves it, it comes in similar guise as to Novalis: in a vision that links his mother and the Virgin Mary. He has earned pardon and redemption through two selfless acts of love: the sacrifice of his ring to stop the threatening deluge, and then his charitable devotion to the cataleptic young soldier. Thereafter Nerval feels 'purifié de mes fautes' ('cleansed of my sins') and as confident as Novalis 'de l'immortalité et de la coexistence de toutes les personnes que j'avais aimées' ('of the immortality and coexistence of all the people I had loved' – i, 413).

These two works thus have a similar religious undercurrent and aura. Novalis and Nerval in fact shared an interest in the occult, in mystical experience, from childhood onwards. Novalis' family was steeped in, the Pietism of the Herrenhut group (his father was reputed to have had visions), while Nerval was nurtured on the works of Cagliostro and Mesmer which he found in his uncle's library. Here too, however, some divergence becomes apparent: for Novalis remained within the Pietist tradition and, therefore, had none of those difficulties in accepting religious revelation of which Nerval complains, and which he attributes to the liberal tendencies of his upbringing. This background, together with his sense of guilt, may account for Nerval's agitation, his periodic lack of faith and his constant recourse to reason in the face of revelation in contrast to Novalis' calm, his fervent belief, and his immediate, unquestioning acceptance of the transcendental. Novalis' journey from despair to belief is a hallowed ascension; that of Nerval leads through 'une descente aux enfers' ('a descent into hell' – i, 414).

There is a further major similarity between the *Hymnen* and *Aurélia* in their use of imagery, specifically patterns of thematic images. The *Hymnen* consist of an intricate counterpoint of two contrasting complexes of related images. Like the themes of a symphony, the two main motifs are enunciated in the first two paragraphs of the cycle. The opening section centres on the idea of light: the word 'Licht' itself stands in an emphatic position at the climax of the initial phrase:

Welcher Lebendige, Sinnbegabte, liebt nicht vor allen Wundererscheinungen des verbreiteten Raums um ihn, das allerfreuliche Licht – mit seinen Farben, seinen Strahlen und
Wogen; seiner milden Allgegenwart, als weckender Tag.

(What living creature, endowed with all his senses, does not
love more than all the marvellous things around him the joys
of light – light with its colours, its rays and waves; its gentle
presence throughout the waking day.)

Here, at the outset, light is associated with day, wakefulness and
life, and its primary role is underlined by the similes with which
the following two sentences begin: 'Wie des Lebens innerste
Seele' ('As the very soul of life') and 'Wie ein König der irdischen
Natur' ('As king over earthly nature'). The whole paragraph
teems with verbs and adjectives of movement, sound and colour
that convey the sheer energy of life inherent in light. Night, the
opposite pole, forms the subject of the second section, but not its
gloomy or frightening aspects. Night is holy ('heilig'), mysterious ('geheimnisvoll') and alluring, in contrast to the emptiness of
the daylight world in the eyes of the bereaved poet. The two sets
of images are linked in the final paragraph of the first *Hymn* when
Novalis makes his decisive inversion of values, choosing night
for his true life because of the visions it brings. Thus the beloved
is called the 'liebliche Sonne der Nacht' ('pleasing sun of the
night'), and many of the terms previously attributed to light are
now applied to night: 'erfreulich' ('joyous'), 'kräftig' ('vigorous'), 'leuchtend' ('shining'), 'wachen' ('wake'), 'Augen'
('eyes'), 'blitzende Sterne' ('sparkling stars'). These are allied to
the words associated with night, such as 'heilig' ('holy') and
'unaussprechlich' ('inexpressible') in a sequence of extraordinary
density. So, by means of a pattern of words and images that
become symbolical, Novalis conveys the cardinal idea of the
Hymnen: 'du hast die Nacht mir zum Leben verkündet' ('you
have revealed night to be my life').

This central theme and its two image-complexes run through
all the subsequent *Hymns* where they are extended and elaborated. The pairs of opposites are sharply contrasted in the
second *Hymn*: 'Morgen' ('morning') against 'Nacht' ('night'),
'irdisch' ('earthly') against 'himmlisch' ('heavenly'), 'Geschäftigkeit' ('activity') against 'heiliger Schlaf' ('holy sleep'),

'Tagewerk' ('daylight work') against 'Liebe' ('love'), 'Zeit zugemessen' ('measured in time') against 'zeitlos' ('timeless'), 'verzehrt' ('consumed') against 'beglücken' ('fulfil'). A new series of images in the latter part of the second *Hymn* illustrating the omnipresence of sleep and death has a direct verbal connection with the first *Hymn*, where the same terms – 'Flut' ('flow'), 'Wunder' ('wonder'), 'Mohn' ('poppies') – had already occurred. The web thickens in the third *Hymn* when images of birth are superimposed on those repeated from the first two *Hymns*: 'das Band der Geburt' ('the umbilical cord') is torn and replaced by 'ein funkelndes unzerreissliches Band' ('a shining lasting link') fashioned out of the tears that unite the poet with his beloved. As the revaluation progresses, the worth of life and light is undermined through words clearly negative in connotation: 'kraftlos' ('weak'), 'in Schmerz aufgelöst' ('dissolved in pain'), 'des Lichtes Fessel' ('the bonds of light'), 'fliehenden, verlöschten Leben' ('fleeing, extinguished life'), 'bittre Tränen' ('bitter tears'). Night, on the other hand, is exalted in ardent terms: 'Nachtbegeisterung' ('ecstasy of night'), 'Himmel der Nacht und sein Licht, die Geliebte' ('heaven of night and its light, the beloved'). The same vocabulary and image patterns pervade the fourth and fifth *Hymns*, in which the parallel between Sophie and Jesus, the poet's personal experience and that of mankind, is further reinforced by the phraseology. The pre-Christian world is now described in the grim terms already associated with the rejected realm of night, while the redeemed era of Christianity with its acceptance of death and after-life has strong linguistic echoes of the positive, joyful reassessments made by Novalis after his revelatory vision. Many of these motifs are woven into the concluding *Hymn* too. It is this interweaving of recurrent images that holds the *Hymnen an die Nacht* together as a poetic cycle with a well articulated structure in spite of its seemingly artless, fluid movement. As the images assume symbolic significance, they become vital carriers of meaning in a manner that was certainly beyond compare in 1800.

Aurélia is also rich in imagery of this kind, although it is perhaps not organised as systematically as in the *Hymnen*. The double view ('aspect double' – i, 381) of life, to which Nerval repeatedly refers, is apparent in the dual images that fill his visions. He sees either an ideal realm, a 'vision céleste' ('a heavenly vision' – i, 364), generally an idyllic scene out of his own past, or a horrendous nightmarish phantasmagoria. In both cases, the evocation of the images alternates between realistic precision, including details of sight, sound and smell, and a shadowy, emblematic suggestiveness. But whatever the mode of presentation, each set of visions is formed into a distinct entity through the recurrence of certain words and motifs. In the ideal realm it is the mother, the divinity or angel, smiles, light and whiteness, luxuriant flowers, 'céleste' ('heavenly'), 'radieux' ('radiant') and 'gracieux' ('graceful'). In the frightening fantasies of suffering, struggle and disaster that break in on Nerval with increasing frequency and vehemence, the leitmotifs are essentially destructive in nature: monsters, fire, flood, combat, withering vegetation, and the keywords are 'maudit' ('accursed') and 'fatal' ('fated'). These images of disruption begin when Nerval becomes aware of Aurélia's death; the connection with Nerval's sense of guilt is obvious. The visions of happiness that dominate the early part of the work return only at the end when he is redeemed. His tendency to see the past and the future in images of good or evil reflects his central preoccupation with the question: 'Suis-je le bon? suis-je le mauvais?' ('Am I the good? am I the evil? – i, 381). Thus the images in *Aurélia* are not only governed by a polarity strikingly reminiscent of the *Hymnen*; they, too, become symbolic carriers of meaning that illustrate and express the underlying theme of the whole work.

It is this use of symbolic imagery, more than any particular stylistic quality, that marks both the *Hymnen* and *Aurélia* as prose-poems. 'The distance between poetical prose and the prose-poem', as Mansell Jones has pointed out,[18] 'is one of degree rather than kind.' And it is ultimately a fundamental difference in organisation, not a question of metrical arrangement: the logical sequence of direct statements that make prose, as against the imaginative transfiguration that underlies poetry and that precipitates the intuitive association of images. So the prose-poem is 'impassioned prose',[19] in which 'elements of rhythm, imagination and feeling are fused in paragraphs of high intensity or concentration.'[20] By these criteria, both the *Hymnen* and *Aurélia* belong to this genre. The *Hymnen* fluctuate between the conventional lay-out of prose in complete lines and the division into short lines customary in poetry. In Novalis' original manuscript they were set out almost entirely in verse although they were subsequently published in the *Athenäum* in a prose version. Not that the typographic arrangement is of any intrinsic importance; whether the words are printed in prose or in verse shape, the approach and expression of the *Hymnen* are throughout those of poetry: the central role of imagery, the fluid association of ideas, the musical element, the lofty vocabulary, the predominance of short phrases that avoid cumbersome dependent clauses, the frequent use of inversion, of compact genitive constructions, of double adjectives and of neologisms: all these belong to poetry, and all occur even in the most sober parts of the *Hymnen*, such as the historical survey at the beginning of the fifth *Hymn*:

Über der Menschen weitverbreitete Stämme herrschte vor Zeiten ein eisernes Schicksal mit stummer Gewalt. Eine dunkle, schwere Binde lag um ihre bange Seele – Unendlich war die Erde – der Götter Aufenthalt, und ihre Heimat. Seit Ewigkeiten stand ihr geheimnisvoller Bau. Über des Morgens roten Bergen, in des Meeres heiligem Schoss wohnte die Sonne, das allzündende, lebendige Licht.

(Over the widely scattered tribes of men an iron fate reigned in ancient times with silent force. A dark, heavy fetter lay on their woebegone souls – infinite was the earth – the Gods' abode and home. Since all eternity their mysterious configuration had endured. Above the red mountains of morning, in the hallowed womb of the ocean dwelt the sun, the all-kindling, living light.)

When, a few lines later, a shift is made into verse, it is a natural transition without any stylistic break. Similarly, the prose of *Aurélia* is to a high degree poetic:

Une perle d'argent brillait dans le sable; une perle d'or étincelait au ciel . . . Le monde était créé. Chastes amours, divins soupirs! enflammez la sainte montagne . . . car vous avez des frères dans les vallées et des soeurs timides qui se dérobent au sein des bois! (i, 409)

(A silver pearl shone in the sand; a golden pearl sparkled in the sky . . . the world was created. Pure love, divine sighs! set the holy mountain alight . . . for you have brothers in the valleys and blushing sisters hiding in the depths of the forests!)

It is worth recalling in this context that Nerval used such musical poetic prose for his rendering of poems by Heine in *Poèmes et Légendes*. That he was aware of the German precedent in this technique is shown by his comment in *Angélique* that 'il est possible de ne pas rimer en poésie; – c'est ce que savent les Allemands, qui dans certaines pièces, emploient seulement les longues et les brèves, à la manière antique.' ('it is possible not to rhyme in poetry; – that is known to the Germans, who, in certain pieces, use only longs and shorts, like the Ancients.' – i, 216).

The essentially poetic character of the *Hymnen* and of *Aurélia* accounts for certain traits of both works that have provoked puzzlement and criticism. Béguin, for instance, writes of the 'incohérence chronologique du récit d'*Aurélia*'[21] ('the disjointed time-sequence of the narrative in *Aurélia*'); this disturbed Symons too.[22] The chronology of the *Hymnen* is equally perplexing, for the third *Hymn* is so closely allied to the first that the intervention of the second seems intrusive. In part the temporal mobility of both works reflects their basic theme: the revaluation of all values from the new perspective of the crucial revelation; the reordering of a whole life in the light of a central crisis. So there is inevitably movement backwards and forwards. But basically the fluidity of these works stems from their *poetic* nature. They both present a story, a narrative of an experience, admittedly esoteric and highly personal; yet at the same time they evoke a mood, capturing an elusive, fleeting atmosphere of the mind. In this fusion of the epic and the lyric, the *Hymnen* and *Aurélia* body forth that duality that is their very subject.

*   *   *   *   *

That this affinity between the *Hymnen* and *Aurélia* should so far have escaped critical attention is surprising, particularly in view of the considerable amount of research devoted to Nerval's relationship to things German.[23] Nerval's importance as an intermediary between Germany and France has long been recognised.[24] Apart from Goethe's *Faust*, Nerval translated works by Schiller, Körner, Jean-Paul, Bürger, Klopstock, Rückert, Heine and Hoffmann; he was also among the first to introduce Wagner into France in an article that forms part of *Loreley*[25] and that was later reprinted in the *Revue Wagnérienne* of 1887.

The German sources of *Aurélia* have been investigated with great thoroughness: Audiat[26] discerns the imprint of *Faust*, of Hoffmann's tales *Der goldene Topf* and *Die Königsbraut*, and of Bürger's *Lenore*, to which Richer[27] has recently added Klopstock and Jean-Paul. What is more, on several occasions the name of Novalis has been linked to that of Nerval. 'Nerval nous apparaît comme un véritable inspiré', writes Richer,[28] 'et, à cet égard, l'égal d'un Blake ou d'un Novalis.' ('Nerval strikes us as a genuine mystic, and in this respect as comparable to a Blake or a Novalis.') Likewise, Vordtriede in his study of the French Symbolists' relationship to Novalis, places Nerval among the so-called 'poets of night' ('Nächtigen'[29]), that is, alongside Novalis. Nerval's 'debt to German practice from Novalis to Hoffmann'[30] is mentioned also by Lehmann, unfortunately only in a brief footnote without further elaboration. Above all, it is Béguin who repeatedly and tantalisingly seems to hover on the very brink of comparison in such comments as: 'S'emparer de son mal, comme put le faire un Novalis et comme le tenta désespérément un Nerval . . .'[31] ('To master one's disorder, as Novalis was able to do and as Nerval desperately tried . . .'); or: 'Comme le Novalis des *Hymnes à la Nuit*, comme le Nerval d'*Aurélia*, Rimbaud ne distingue pas entre son "rêve" et sa "vie"'[32] ('Like the Novalis of the *Hymns to the Night*, like the Nerval of *Aurélia*, Rimbaud draws no distinction between his "dream" and his "life"'). But in his analysis of *Aurélia*, Béguin, somewhat disappointingly, does not go beyond this rhetorical question, added in parenthesis: 'et comment ne pas songer à Novalis?'[33] ('and how can one help thinking of Novalis?'). Only Charles Dédéyan has attempted more: in chapter XXI of his *Gérard de Nerval et l'Allemagne* (Paris: Société d'édition d'enseignement supérieur, 1957–9) under the heading 'Novalis ou les affinités mystiques' he has pinpointed the various themes common to Nerval and Novalis: the loss of the beloved, the mother–figure, night, the grotto, the flower, the subterranean realm, the search for harmony, and so forth. Yet this piecemeal method tends to produce a mass of details rather than any coherent, meaningful conclusions.

The one factor which has – and not without reason – deterred comparison of the *Hymnen* and *Aurélia* is the lack of evidence of any outer link between Novalis and Nerval. It seems impossible to establish with any certainty whether Nerval was acquainted with the writings of Novalis or not. Novalis' name never occurs in either Nerval's correspondence or in *Loreley*, an account of his travels in Germany, in which he does refer to Goethe, Schiller, Herder, Wieland, Kotzebue, Heine, Körner, Hoffmann and Klinger. There is, therefore, some justification for Richer's question: 'Comment croire que, si Nerval avait bien connu W. Blake, Beckford ou Novalis, il n'en aurait pas longuement parlé?'[34] ('How are we to believe that if Nerval had been really familiar with Blake, Beckford or Novalis, he would not have spoken about them at length?')

In favour of the opposite view – that Nerval must surely have known Novalis – there is an accumulation of circumstantial evidence. Novalis' works were quite readily available in Paris after their publication in 1837 by Têtot Frères. Moreover, it is highly unlikely that Nerval never came across the name of Novalis in the course either of his travels or of his work as a translator who handled a wide range of German poetry of just that period. Nerval also had ample opportunity to hear about Novalis in Paris through both articles and personal contacts: in 1831 Montalembert published a long essay on Novalis in *L'Avenir*; the *Nouvelle Revue Germanique* of 1834 contained a biography of Novalis as well as a version of the *Hymnen* by Xavier Marmier, whom Nerval is known to have respected as an authority on German literature; and the first of a series of articles on German lyric poetry in the *Revue des Deux Mondes* of 1841–5 included a paraphrase of chapter 5 (the descent into the mine) of *Heinrich von Ofterdingen*. These articles were by Henri Blaze de Bury, a friend of Nerval; again it is improbable that Blaze de Bury, who had translated Novalis, should not have spoken of his work to his friend and fellow-translator. There are still further possibilities in Nerval's friendship and collaboration with Heine, who came to Paris in 1831 and who certainly knew of Novalis. Loève-Weimars, who published a *Résumé de l'histoire de la littéra- ture allemande* in 1826, and Koreff, a friend of Hoffmann, pro- vided more contacts. Tenuous though each of these links may be in itself, taken together they add up to a considerable weight of testimony. There is at least a strong likelihood that Nerval was aware of Novalis' works. This seems indeed to be a common assumption of some recent critics who, without any apparent hesitation, make such statements as this: 'as a Germanist translator of *Faust* at the age of eighteen, Nerval is probably thinking here of the opening pages of Novalis' *Die Lehrlinge zu Saïs.*'[35]

But even if there is, as I believe, enough evidence to warrant the supposition that Nerval was familiar with the works of Novalis, this is hardly a sufficient foundation on which to conjecture any influence. To surmise that Nerval had heard of Novalis and had very possibly read some of his writing seems a justifiable proposition; to postulate, however, that Novalis influenced Nerval is no more than a speculation unsupported by facts. This is the crux of the problem that has perhaps discouraged comparison of these two poets. But the establishment of a direct influence is by no means the only purpose of such a juxtaposition. The multi-faceted similarity between the *Hymnen* and *Aurélia* proves in fact to have a significance of far greater import.

That significance becomes apparent when these two works are considered from a slightly different angle, not only in relation to each other, but also from the perspective of the literatures in which they stand. The position of the *Hymnen* in the history of German literature is clear: they mark the triumphant breakthrough of Romanticism, fulfilling for the first time the demands Friedrich Schlegel had been making for the new poetry. Their originality and poetic potency remain unequalled. The *Hymnen* are a decisive document in the evolution of German literature because they speak with a voice unheard before: radically subjective in its total reliance on an esoteric inner experience, truly imaginative and musical in its texture of symbolic imagery.

The place of *Aurélia* in French literature is rather harder to define. Nerval's writings have always defied classification. For a time he was put among the minor Romantics; but – leaving aside the value judgement implied in 'minor' – his affiliation to the mainstream of French Romanticism is very questionable. Nerval's poetry is perceptibly different in approach and manner from that of, say, Lamartine or Musset. This is particularly evident in *Aurélia*, Nerval's last work. It is difficult to site within French literature because it was so unconventional, indeed so revolutionary. As Béguin has pointed out:

La prose d'*Aurélia* et les quelques sonnets des *Chimères* appartiennent à une poésie qui est sans exemple dans l'histoire des lettres françaises: non seulement parce qu'il y est fait des mots, des images, des allusions, un choix et un usage tout nouveaux, mais aussi et surtout parce que l'attitude de l'écrivain devant son oeuvre et les espoirs qu'il lui confie sont ici très différents de tout ce que l'on avait encore vu.[36]

(The prose of *Aurélia* and the few sonnets of the *Chimères* belong to a poetry unprecedented in the history of French literature: not only because words, images and allusions are chosen and used in a wholly novel manner, but also and above all because the poet's attitude to his work and the hopes he invests in it are very different from anything that had been witnessed hitherto.)

With these words, as appropriate to the *Hymnen* as to *Aurélia*, the similarity between the two works is once again underscored.

They occupy analogous positions in their respective literatures insofar as both mark an important new departure. First, they are milestones of *romantisme intérieur* because their subjectivity differs in kind, as well as in degree, from that of their predecessors. But their ultimate significance as key works goes far beyond this. For the *Hymnen* and *Aurélia* are gateways to Symbolism in their special use of imagery, which foreshadows that of their successors. They attempt to communicate unique personal feeling by 'a complicated association of ideas represented by a medley of metaphors',[37] to quote Edmund Wilson's summary of Symbolist technique. They seek not to inform but to suggest and evoke, not to name things but to create their atmosphere, as Mallarmé and Stefan George later wished. They convey fleeting, indefinite states of mind in poetic prose as rich in harmonies as in images. They are fundamentally mystical in claiming greater validity for an ideal inner world than for the outer world of the senses. And they have that peculiar intensity and excitement that emanates from Symbolist poetry at its best.

Here then are two works that must certainly be deemed 'incomparable' when seen simply in the context of their native literary tradition. They are, however, eminently comparable to each other in respect of their intrinsic characteristics and, equally, of the crucial turning-point which each marks. That their dates of publication are some fifty years apart is in itself of some consequence. For the *Hymnen* and *Aurélia* indicate the moment when the creative imagination attained unchallenged sovereignty in their respective literatures. This happened appreciably earlier in Germany than in France. In German Romanticism the autonomous imagination of the divine artist already achieved a supremacy that is without parallel in the French Romanticism of the early nineteenth century. Nerval himself recognised this when he wrote: 'chez nous c'est l'homme qui gouverne son imagination; chez les Allemands c'est l'imagination qui gouverne l'homme'[38] ('with us it is man who dominates the imagination; with the Germans it is the imagination that dominates man'). This was true enough until then; but with *Aurélia* the imagination began to be as assertive in France as it had long been in Germany. Herein, rather than in any specific influence or borrowing, lies the quintessence of Nerval's heritage from Germany. And herein also lies the patrimony of the French Symbolists from the German Romantics who had grasped as early as the first years of the nineteenth century that 'das Schöne ist eine symbolische Darstellung des Unendlichen'[39] ('the beautiful is a symbolic representation of the infinite'), thereby laying the foundation stone of European Symbolism.[40]

NOTES TO CHAPTER 7

1. Paul Kluckhohn, 'Romantische Dichtung', in *Romantik*, ed. T. Stein-büchel (Tubingen: Rainer Wunderlich, 1948) p. 48.
2. Friedrich Hiebel, *Novalis, der Dichter der blauen Blume* (Bern: Francke, 1951) p. 170.
3. H. A. Korff, *Geist der Goethezeit* (Leipzig: Koehler & Amelang, 1940), vol. iii, p. 541.
4. Rudolf Haym, *Die romantische Schule* (Berlin: Gaertner, 1870) p. 336.
5. Paul Kluckhohn, *Die deutsche Romantik* (Bielefeld and Liepzig: Velhagen and Klasing, 1924) p. 199.
6. Korff, *Geist der Goethezeit*, vol. iii, p. 536.
7. Theophile Gautier, Preface to *Le Rêve et la vie*; cited by Pierre Audiat, *L'"Aurélia" de Gérard de Nerval* (Paris: Champion, 1926) p. 5.
8. Albert Béguin, *L'Âme romantique et le rêve* (Paris: Corti, 1939) p. 358.
9. Arthur Symons, *The Symbolist Movement in Literature* (London: Heinemann, 1899) p. 19.
10. Percy Mansell Jones, *The Background of Modern French Poetry* (Cambridge: Cambridge Univ. Press, 1951) p. 108.
11. Solomon Alhadeb Rhodes, *Gérard de Nerval* (London: Peter Owen – Vision Press, 1952) p. 365.
12. Otto Weise, *Gérard de Nerval: Romantik und Symbolismus* (Halle:

Akademischer Verlag, 1936) p. 121.

13. Béguin, *L'Âme romantique et le rêve*, p. 358.
14. Aristide Marie, *Gérard de Nerval* (Paris: Hachette, 1914) p. 332.
15. Gérard de Nerval, *Oeuvres*, ed. Albert Béguin and Jean Richer (Paris: Gallimard, 1952) vol. i, p. 392. All subsequent references are to this edition.
16. Symons, *The Symbolist Movement in Literature*, p. 6.
17. Béguin, *L'Âme romantique et le rêve*, p. 360.
18. Mansell Jones, *The Background of Modern French Poetry*, p. 97.
19. Mansell Jones, *The Background of Modern French Poetry*, p. 99.
20. Mansell Jones, *The Background of Modern French Poetry*, p. 97.
21. Béguin, *L'Âme romantique et le rêve*, p. 360.
22. Symons, *The Symboiist Movement in Literature*, pp. 28–9.
23. For a survey of the *état présent* in this field see Alfred Dubruck, *Gérard de Nerval and the German Heritage* (The Hague: Mouton, 1955) pp. 11–42.
24. As early as 1904 Julia Cartier sub-titled her study of Nerval: *Un Intermédiaire entre la France et l'Allemagne* (Geneva: Société générale d'Imprimerie, 1904).
25. Nerval, *Oeuvres* vol. ii, pp. 794–7.
26. Audiat, *L'"Aurélia' de Gérard de Nerval*, pp. 47–52.
27. Jean Richer, *Nerval: expérience et création* (Paris: Hachette, 1963) pp. 447–52.
28. Richer, *Nerval*, p. 23.
29. Werner Vordtriede, *Novalis und die französischen Symbolisten* (Stuttgart: Kohlhammer, 1963) p. 151.
30. Andrew George Lehmann, *The Symbolist Aesthetic in France 1885–1895* (Oxford: Blackwell, 1950) p. 87 footnote.
31. Béguin, *L'Âme romantique et le rêve*, p. 28.
32. Béguin, *L'Âme romantique el le rêve*, p. 387.
33. Béguin, *L'Âme romantique et le rêve*, p. 359.
34. Richer, *Nerval*, p. 463.
35. Gwendolyn M. Bays, 'Nerval, Baudelaire and Rimbaud', *Comparative Literature Studies*, iv, Nos. 1 & 2 (1967) 22.
36. Béguin, *L'Âme romantique et le rêve*, p. 358.
37. Edmund Wilson, *Axel's Castle* (New York: Scribner's 1931) pp. 21–2.
38. Nerval, *Poésies allemandes* (Paris: Dumont, 1830) p. 35.
39. August Wilhelm Schlegal, *Vorlesungen über schöne Kunst und Literatur, Kritische Schriften und Briefe*, ed. Edgar Lohner (Stuttgart: Kohlhammer, 1963) vol. ii (Die Kunstlehre) p. 81.
40. See also Lilian R. Furst, *Counterparts: The Dynamics of Franco-German Literary Relationships 1770–1895* (London: Methuen, and Detroit: Wayne State Univ. Press, 1977) pp. 99–173.

8 The Configuration of Romantic Agony

'Why, after all, should the same movement have led from Sir Galahad to *Salome*, from the Lady of the Lake to *La Charogne*, from chivalry to sadistic tortures, from idealism to ordure?' The question is posed with characteristic trenchancy by F. L. Lucas in the epilogue – 'for reviewers and others who may find the book too long' – to *The Decline and Fall of the Romantic Ideal*.[1] The line of continuity between the Romantic movement of the late eighteenth and early nineteenth centuries and the Decadence of the latter half of the nineteenth century has long been recognised. But what is their relationship, or rather, the nature of the development that led from the one to the other? A number of hypotheses have been put forward.

Lucas himself favoured a Freudian interpretation that cast Realism in the role of the ego, Classicism in that of the superego, and Romanticism as the id. Following this scheme, Romanticism was branded an 'intoxicated dreaming' (p. 46) that could – and did – all too easily lead to the delirium tremens of Sensationalism, Satanism and Sadism when the stimulant had to be varied and the dose increased to the point of exaggeration, frenzy, and disease. Adducing Chateaubriand's image, Lucas graphically refers to the dangers of the unconscious, unleashed when Romanticism lifted the hatches, as 'the Crocodiles of Alachua', crocodiles that fascinated and even entertained, but eventually gobbled up the Decadents. So the Romantic, 'wandering in the woods of dream, has often wandered too far, and got lost' (p. 278), Lucas concludes. He sees the relationship between Romanticism and Decadence as a 'decline and fall' propelled like an avalanche by its own gathering momentum.

On this point Mario Praz, the populariser of what he called 'Romantic Agony', is less specific than Lucas. Praz has curiously little interest in the process of evolution, nor even any strong awareness of the time factor. He slips like a yo-yo up and down the nineteenth century, occasionally dipping into the eighteenth or overshooting into the twentieth. In a parenthesis in the opening sentence of *The Romantic Agony* (London and New York: Oxford University Press, 1933) he states that 'the Decadent movement of the end of the last century is only a development' of Romanticism, without in any way further specifying that development. His primary focus, as he concedes in the foreword to the first edition, is on 'the darker portions of the picture', especially the erotic sensibility. It is well to recall that the book's original title was *La carne, la morte e il diavolo nella letteratura romantica* (The Flesh, Death and the Devil in Romantic Literature); it is a catalogue of certain aberrant tendencies latent in Romanticism and prominent in Decadence.

In contrast to Praz, two more recent critics have been concerned mainly with the dynamics of the nineteenth century, and thus inevitably with the relationship of Romanticism to Decadence. K. W. Swart's *The Sense of Decadence in Nineteenth-Century France* treats literature as an accessory to the exploration of political, social and philosophical trends. Swart perceives the nineteenth century as torn between hope and despair; suffering great disillusionment, even disaster; aware of its degeneracy, yet constantly buoyed by a belief in progress that was buttressed by the advance of science. Against this background, Decadence emerges as a fusion of three major strands: 'the Romantic cult of modernism, estheticism and individualism to greater extremes'[2]; the weary disillusionment characteristic of the period; and such outside influences as the philosophy of Schopenhauer. Swart's view departs from that of Lucas insofar as he approaches the problem from another angle, but in the last resort he too regards Decadence as an intensified continuation of Romanticism.

A somewhat different concept is found in A. E. Carter's *The Idea of Decadence in French Literature 1830–1900*. Carter does not envisage Decadence merely as a variant on Romanticism plus – or minus – certain factors, although he still considers it 'a final development'[3] of Romanticism, which 'degenerated very lushly and very soon' (p. 147). But he distinguishes Decadence sharply from Romanticism in that cult of artificiality which, according to Carter, is its salient feature. This emphasis on artificiality leads Carter to his thesis that Decadence is 'primitivism – *à rebours*'

(p. 4), 'orthodox Rousseauism turned inside out' (p. 20). Decadence, he maintains, 'was in revolt against Romantic theory on two essential points – the cult of Nature and the cult of ideal love. Its artificiality contradicts both; it begins (in De Sade and Baudelaire) as a renunciation of Rousseau's naturism, and develops into the practice of whatever can be thought anti-natural and abnormal' (p. 150).

Carter's arguments are convincing and stimulating, though in the last analysis not wholly satisfying. Possibly the reservation may stem from his all too ready equation of Romanticism with primitivism, and Decadence with artificiality. Such a simplification does violence to complex clusters of ideas by taking *pars pro toto*. But this objection in no way invalidates his fundamental hypothesis that Decadence is a development of Romanticism somehow *à rebours* (upside down). This is the notion that I propose to explore through a comparison of Novalis' *Heinrich von Ofterdingen* (1802) and Huysmans' aptly named *A Rebours* (1884), works that stand at opposite ends of the nineteenth century as the quintessence of Romanticism and Decadence respectively.

★   ★   ★   ★   ★

In spite of the eighty or so years between their dates of publication, numerous parallelisms in form as well as in theme link *Heinrich von Ofterdingen* and *A Rebours*. At the same time, however, this framework of similarities serves to reveal all the more sharply the deep divergences.

In form both works are closer to the prose poem than to the traditional novel. Plot is largely subsidiary to the evocation of mood and atmosphere, while the use of language is governed by aesthetic rather than functional considerations. This poetic timbre is a direct outcome of both authors' avowed intentions. Novalis, who regarded the novel as akin to the *Märchen* and concurred with Friedrich Schlegel's punning definition of the *Roman* (novel) as 'ein romantisches Buch'[4] ('a romantic book'), was deliberately fashioning an anti-*Wilhelm Meister*; his *Heinrich von Ofterdingen* was conceived as an imaginative apotheosis of *Poesie*. Huysmans was even more outspoken in his opposition to the dominant excessively pedestrian mode. In the 1903 preface to

A Rebours he recalls that by the early 1880s Naturalism seemed to be heading for 'une impasse', and that 'Je cherchais vaguement à m'évader d'un cul-de-sac où je suffoquais'[5] ('I was somehow looking for a way out of a dead-end where I was suffocating'). The programme he outlines for his work is remarkably close to the *Frühromantik* concept of the novel: 'de briser les limites du roman, d'y faire entrer l'art, la science, l'histoire, de ne plus se servir, en un mot, de cette forme que comme d'un cadre pour y insérer de plus sérieux travaux.' ('to break the bounds of the novel, to bring into it art, science, history, in other words, to use this form only as a frame into which to insert more serious work.' – p. 40). This is strongly reminiscent of the *Frühromantik* ideal of a universal art form that would gradually embrace all aspects of human life. In both instances the aim was an expansion of the traditional novel in favour of a fluid amplitude.

Yet within their poetic continuity, the two works also have a pseudo-picaresque structure. Each consists of a string-like succession of the hero's experiences. The episodes show a certain progression from beginning to end, although their actual order could be shuffled without substantially altering the works, specially in the middle. For instance, Heinrich could meet the miner or the hermit before Zulima, while the sequence of Des Esseintes' experiments with perfumes, jewels, flowers and so on seems fairly arbitrary. The individual episodes in the hero's epiphany are relatively self-contained and independent of one another, though each contributes to his cumulative experience of the world. The technique is the same in *Heinrich von Ofterdingen* and *A Rebours*, namely the extensive use of insertions into a flexible framework. Klingsohr's *Märchen*, the merchants' tales, and the encounters with Zulima, the miner and the hermit in *Heinrich von Ofterdingen* have their counterparts in *A Rebours* in the episodes with Auguste, Miss Urania, the journey to England, and the religious and literary meditations. No wonder that Emile Hennequin, in his review of *A Rebours* in the *Revue indépendante* (i, 1884), raised the question as to whether the virtuosity of the parts did not detract from the totality of the work. That question is equally pertinent to *Heinrich von Ofterdingen*. It is this independence of the sections that leads to the dualistic organisation of the two works: the separate parts form a series of encapsulated entities that are held together by the picaresque thread.

The material inserted within the framework is, however, significantly different in the two novels. In both there are some lyrics; but in *A Rebours* these are quotations from poets that Des Esseintes particularly admires (Baudelaire, Mallarmé, Verlaine), whereas in *Heinrich von Ofterdingen* they are newly created poems. Similarly, the fables that Heinrich experiences, though they draw on traditional folk-tales, show a greater degree of inventiveness than the critical activity in which Des Esseintes is immersed. This difference already points to the antithesis between the productive and the reproductive, between Heinrich the budding poet and Des Esseintes the dessicating aesthete. The dichotomy extends indeed to the two works as a whole, revealing the gulf between the Romantic orientation to the future and to creativity as against the Decadent fixation on the past that can become an impeding burden.

This pattern of divergence within similarity is repeated in the thematic motifs. Both novels depict a young man in search of his place in the world, of his role and his identity. The element of the *Bildungsroman* is quite plainly apparent in *Heinrich von Ofterdingen*, rather more obliquely so in *A Rebours*. The two protagonists are alike in their initial malaise in their present state, although Des Esseintes' dissatisfaction is far more intense. With Heinrich it is mainly the disgruntledness of adolescence, which is alleviated by his mother's decision to take him on a journey to his grandfather in Augsburg. That journey proves as much metaphorical as literal, for in the course of this first foray into the world Heinrich makes the gradual discovery of his poetic calling. In keeping with the temper of the *Frühromantik*, Heinrich's quest is lofty, and it is sustained by a buoyant sense of hope and excitement. Des Esseintes, on the other hand, in the post-Byronic age, is impelled by the need to escape from the 'immense ennui' ('overpowering tedium' – p. 55) that has brought him to the verge of suicide. His strong aversion to modern society is allied to a hatred of nature that leaves him few alternatives. So, in contrast to the positive ideal that inspires Heinrich's journey, the impetus for Des Esseintes' venture is the negative one of despair. The Romantic quest has quasi-religious overtones; the Decadent verges on the tragi-comic.

The direction of that quest takes both Heinrich and Des Esseintes away from their immediate surroundings into a new world. *A Rebours* opens with the move to Fontenay-aux-Roses, where Des Esseintes makes a conscious, calculated effort to create for himself that 'irdisches Paradies'[6] ('terrestrial paradise') that Heinrich finds so readily around and within him. Herein perhaps lies the Decadent's ultimate tragedy: that he so doggedly seeks – and fails ever to find – that incarnation of the ideal that seems to offer itself so spontaneously to the Romantic. Des Esseintes in fact treads all the byways familiar to Heinrich: there is 'un retour aux âges consommés, aux civilisations disparues, aux temps morts; . . . un élancement vers le fantastique et le rêve, . . . une vision plus ou moins intense d'un temps à éclore dont l'image reproduit, sans qu'il le sache, par un effet d'atavisme, celle des époques révolues' ('a return to past ages, to vanished civilisations, to dead centuries; . . . a pursuit of fantasy and dream, a more or less vivid vision of a future whose image reproduces, unconsciously and as a result of atavism, that of past epochs' – p. 280). What Des Esseintes desires, Heinrich comes to possess. Like *A Rebours*, *Heinrich von Ofterdingen* begins at the dawn of a new world that is foreshadowed in Heinrich's dream in the first chapter, a dream that is eventually fulfilled in his union with Mathilde and his exaltation to the realm of *Poesie*. Both Heinrich and Des Esseintes follow the 'Weg der innern Betrachtung' ('path of inner contemplation' – p. 33), the journey into the self, from the mundane earth into the transcendental vision. 'Die Welt wird Traum, der Traum wird Welt' ('the world becomes a dream, the dream becomes world' – p. 181); 'substituer le rêve de la réalité à la réalité même' ('to replace reality itself by the dream of reality' – p. 75): such interplay of reality and dream is the summit of Heinrich's and Des Esseintes' aspirations. But the Decadent's ascent into the dream is only transient, while the Romantic purportedly attains a lasting elevation.

By the end, they have both completed a circular trajectory. Des Esseintes goes literally back to his starting-point, to Paris, where he finds 'son horizon plus menaçant et plus noir' ('his horizon more threatening and darker' – p. 332) than at the outset. His future seems grim. Heinrich's future seems as nebulous as that of Des Esseintes, and *Heinrich von Ofterdingen* as open-ended as *A Rebours* (the second part remained a fragment on Novalis' death). Like Hyazinth in *Die Lehrlinge zu Saïs*, Heinrich gravitates 'immer nach Hause' ('ever homewards' – p. 188). Yet in a sequence of climaxes he is moving upwards into a higher realm, whereas Des Esseintes' homing tendency is downward, a descent in a succession of anti-climaxes.

Thus, the divergences between the two works come to have increasing importance. For instance, the differences between Heinrich and Des Esseintes, marked enough at the beginning, intensify as they develop in opposite directions. Heinrich first appears as a fresh, innocent youth of twenty, forward-looking in his eagerness to embark on life's adventures. Des Esseintes is a bare ten years older, but he is already disillusioned and prematurely spent after tasting – and scorning – the pleasures of life. The waning of his virility is implicit in his appearance; he is a 'grêle jeune homme de trente ans, anémique et nerveux, aux joues caves, aux yeux d'un bleu froid d'acier, au nez éventé et pourtant droit, aux mains sèches et fluettes' ('frail young man of thirty, anemic and highly strung, with hollow cheeks and eyes of a cold steely blue, a nose that was turned up but straight, and slender, dried up hands' – p. 48). Before long he falls victim to a disease that makes him even more cadaverous: 'la figure était couleur de terre, les lèvres boursouflées et sèches, la langue ridée, la peau rugueuse; ses cheveux et sa barbe, que le domestique n'avait plus taillés depuis la maladie, ajoutaient encore à l'horreur de la face creuse, des yeux agrandis et liquoreux qui brûlaient d'un éclat fébrile dans cette tête de squelette' ('his face was earthen in colour, the lips dry and swollen, the tongue cracked, the skin wrinkled; his hair and his beard, which the servant had not trimmed since his illness, further heightened the horrific impression of the hollow cheeks, the big, watery eyes burning with a feverish brightness in this death's head' – p. 316). There is no equivalent physical description of Heinrich – he is an idealised, almost disembodied figure – but his enterprise attests to his healthy vigour. He makes the long journey that Des Esseintes typically shuns, he goes down into the mine, and his awakening sexuality responds with beating heart to the young women he meets. His life is on the rise, as against Des Esseintes' declining proclivity.

That contrast is as evident in the intellectual as in the physical sphere. *Heinrich von Ofterdingen* portrays the hero's growth, the 'Entwickelungen seines ahndungsvollen Innern' ('unfolding of his intuitive inner being' – p. 105). In the form of an outer and inner journey, the novel traces Heinrich's progress to the twofold point of arrival: literally in Augsburg at his grandfather's home, and metaphorically in his meeting with the spirit of poetry, Klingsohr, and Mathilde, his daughter. Throughout, there is a sense of movement that is a reflection of Heinrich's own receptivity to new experiences. Des Esseintes, on the other hand, travels only to Fontenay-aux-Roses and *back*, a very limited and limiting excursion that symbolises his static existence. His review of the objects already in his library, a review that confirms the views he already held, is as symptomatic of his mental stagnation as his last-minute decision not to travel to England. Characteristically, the one occasion on which he actually sallies out into the world ends in a precipitate retreat to Fontenay. The motif of retreat is a recurrent one in *A Rebours*: his house is described as 'sa cellule' ('his cell' – p. 113); his reflex reaction to the vicissitudes of life is a regression into his study ('il se réfugia dans son cabinet de travail' – p. 206), with the result that 'il s'éloignait, de plus en plus, de la réalité et surtout du monde contemporain' ('he became more and more remote from reality, and especially from the contemporary world' – p. 279). This withdrawal from the world is the reverse of Heinrich's entry into the world. Heinrich moves outwards in an ever widening circle, whereas Des Esseintes retires inwards into an increasingly restricted area. The difference is objectified in the opposing images that dominate the two novels: in *Heinrich von Ofterdingen* it is the opening of doors and windows, a continuing admission of light from the awakening at daybreak in the initial pages; on the other hand, in *A Rebours* it is the enclosed darkness of the artificial domain that Des Esseintes has fashioned for himself, and that he fosters in his nocturnal upside-down living.

Likewise, in relationship to people and to things, Heinrich is by instinct open, and Des Esseintes by calculation closed. He withholds as far as possible from any human intercourse; even his two old servants are kept at a distance by elaborate precautions such as thick carpeting, obligatory felt slippers, a code of signals to convey his needs, and for the woman, a special costume inoffensive to his delicate sensibility. Living in this 'rigide silence de moines claustrés, sans communication avec le dehors, dans des pièces aux fenêtres et aux portes closes' ('absolute silence of cloistered monks, without any communication with the outside world, in rooms with closed windows and doors' – p. 69), he is totally insulated from the stream of ordinary activity, for which he feels nothing but scorn and contempt. In contrast to Des Esseintes' cold aloofness, Heinrich delights in a warm and harmonious communion with the world around him. He leaves the cocoon of his family to participate in the life of his time, travelling with a group of merchants and joining gladly in

the festivities at their overnight sojourns. He is always sur-
rounded by people in whom he takes a keen interest, and since he
is a handsome, open-hearted youth, he quickly forms affection-
ate ties to the young women who cross his path. What is more,
most of the people he meets – the miner, the hermit, and
Klingsohr himself – radiate a sense of contentment. Conversely,
in *A Rebours*, as a result of Des Esseintes' isolation and in
reflection of his human atrophy, relatively few characters play
any active part, and they all belong to the past, so that they
appear only in Des Esseintes' memory. Auguste, Miss Urania,
and the lady ventriloquist are weird, dissatisfied creatures. The
choice of such sexual objects is surely telling evidence of Des
Esseintes' perverted mentality even before his retreat.

In their approach to inanimate things Heinrich and Des Esseintes are as different as in their dealings with human beings. For
Heinrich the past is brought to life directly by word of mouth
through the reminiscences of the merchants and the knights; for
Des Esseintes it is evoked only in books. Heinrich comes across
minerals in their natural state through his meeting with the
miner, whereas Des Esseintes will countenance only the rarest
and most refined stones on his tortoise. Thus Heinrich's experiences are consistently immediate and spontaneous; Des Esseintes' are premeditated and contrived. What is particularly
significant, moreover, is that things seem to undergo an antithetical process under Des Esseintes' and Heinrich's touch. The
aesthete, through his own sterility, has a withering effect: the
jewel-studded tortoise dies; so do the bizarre flowers, chosen for
their very appearance of artificiality; even the lascivious body of
Salome in Moreau's picture is somehow robbed of its vibrant
force by the comparison to cold stones: 'sur le corps resté nu,
entre le gorgerin et la ceinture, le ventre bombe, creusé d'un
nombril dont le trou semble un cachet gravé d'onyx' ('the body
shows bare between gorgerin and girdle, the belly bulges out,
dimpled by a navel which resembles a graven seal of onyx' –
p. 120). Under Heinrich's animating gaze, on the other hand,
there is a universal blossoming: the blue flower in his initial
dream comes alive with a girl's face at its centre, and later, all that
he experiences 'stand wie ein klingender Baum voll goldener
Früchte vor ihm' ('stood before him like a resonant tree full of
golden fruits' – p. 117), an organic image that synthesises with
extraordinary economy the vital sensations of sound, sight and
taste. Finally, the contrasting dreams of Heinrich and Des Es-

seintes reveal to the full the polarity between the Romantic and the Decadent: the former's idyll of the blue flower as against the latter's nightmare of the pox.

These heterogeneous modes of dreaming in fact epitomise the opposing directions in which these two characters develop. Des Esseintes' existence is a crescendo of nightmares, moving towards disease, insanity and death. Hollowed out by physical as well as psychological derangement, he realises that the 'croyance en une vie future serait seule apaisante' ('only the belief in a future life could calm him' – p. 334). But since such belief is 'impossible' for him, in his embittered, frustrated anguish he almost revels in the thought of the imminent apocalypse: 'Eh! croule donc, société! meurs donc, vieux monde!' ('Well, crumble then, society! perish, old world!' – p. 333). Nothing could be further removed from this nihilism than the ending of *Heinrich von Ofterdingen* which heralds the approach of the Golden Age in the union of Heinrich and Mathilde, the reign of *Poesie*, and the symbolical marriage of the seasons. Heinrich becomes 'grösser und edler' ('greater and nobler' – p. 107), suffused with 'eine so schöpferische und gediegene Heiterkeit' ('so creative and confident a serenity' – p. 127), the diametric opposite of Des Esseintes' repeated disappointment. All the aesthete's experiments – with the tortoise, with Auguste, with the retreat to Fontenay – have adverse results, while the disposition of *Heinrich von Ofterdingen* is towards a happy outcome. Heinrich has many positive experiences on his journey, he finds Mathilde and Klingsohr, and even in the merchants' tale the lost princess is restored to her father, complete with husband and fine baby! The best formula for the discrepancy between Heinrich and Des Esseintes is found in Klingsohr's words as he sets the 'belebende Wärme eines dichterischen Gemüts' ('animating warmth of a poetic spirit') against 'jener wilden Hitze eines kränklichen Herzens' ('the frenzied vehemence of a morbid heart' – p. 129).

The juxtaposition of *Heinrich von Ofterdingen* and *A Rebours* thus uncovers a pattern of contrasts contained within certain similarities. That pattern points to the fundamental polarity in the ideology underlying the two works. Heinrich's journey is a triumphant mission into the world, rising in an expansive arch to the moment of arrival, of fulfilment, whereas Des Esseintes' solipsistic withdrawal into ever narrower confines leads him only into a dead-end. His course is characterised by non-arrival: each of his projects ends in a crisis, in effect in a failure that further intensifies his pessimism to a nadir of Schopenhauerian nihilism. Appropriately, Robert Adams[7] has sited Des Esseintes as the last stage in the literary conquest of the void during the nineteenth century. For Des Esseintes 'avait bondi sur une fausse piste et erré dans des visions inégalables, ne découvrant nullement sur la terre ce pays magique et réel qu'il espérait' ('had embarked on an erroneous path and strayed amidst unrealisable visions, finding nowhere on earth that truly magic land for which he hoped' – p. 225). It is this recognition that his longings are essentially unattainable that first deters Des Esseintes from his journey to England and eventually drives him into a delirium of despair. The futility of his desires is confirmed by the miscarriage of his endeavours in the face of a recalcitrant reality. The death of his tortoise, so painstakingly studded with recondite jewels that fit perfectly into the carpet and the room, is a striking symbol for the thwarting of his aesthetic ideal. Renouncing hope for the future, Des Esseintes seeks consolation in the past, particularly in the works of art that appeal to him. Or, in his contempt for the normal modes that have failed him, he turns to bizarre perversions in a final, desperate search for satisfaction. But even perversion leads to disappointment, emptiness – in a word, agony. Des Esseintes is finally left facing a blank, sombre wall, while Heinrich gazes out with hope and faith into the future, buoyed by the progressive fulfilment of his dream of love and *Poesie*, and confident of the ultimate apotheosis of the creative imagination. It is idealism that pervades *Heinrich von Ofterdingen*, and agony *A Rebours*.

*   *   *   *   *

To come back then to Lucas' question, as to why the same movement led from Sir Galahad to *Salome*, from the Lady of the Lake to *La Charogne*. By referring to Romanticism and Decadence as 'the same movement', Lucas is clearly predicating a certain line of continuity. The contours of that line are adumbrated in the correlation between *Heinrich von Ofterdingen* and *A Rebours*. Although it would patently be injudicious to draw broad conclusions from a limited base, nevertheless, because *Heinrich von Ofterdingen* represents the summation of early-nineteenth-century transcendental Romanticism just as *A Rebours* does of late-nineteenth-century Decadence, the filiation from the one to the other does at least suggest the trend of development in the course of the century, and, specifically, the nature of the lineage from Romanticism to Decadence.

The comparison of *Heinrich von Ofterdingen* and *A Rebours* supports Carter's thesis that Decadence denotes a reversal of what had gone before. But Carter's assertion, as it stands, is a simplification or at best a partial statement of a fairly complex situation. Decadence is more than merely primitivism *à rebours* in the same way as Des Esseintes is more than 'a photographic negative' of 'the Noble Savage'.[8] For Decadence is at one and the same time a continuation of Romanticism and its reversal. The Romantic quest for the perfect state of being impells the Decadent too, but instead of ever finding fulfilment, the Decadent experiences such repeated frustration and disappointment that he is finally provoked to invert his quest into a subconscious pursuit of self-destruction. So his agony is a parodistic transposition of Romantic idealism. Symptomatic of this is the manner in which the Romantics' high-minded aspirations become tinged, among the Decadents, with a semi-serious playfulness. The work of art that is created with boundless devotion is, in fact, a jewel-studded tortoise – that dies.

This change was neither sudden nor the outcome of a linear, chronological evolution. Although Romantic agony is associated primarily with the later half of the nineteenth century, its features are visible long before, and so is the reversal of idealism into agony. To the extent that idealism and agony may be equated with hope and despair, that reversal can even be considered an archetypal human pattern. Certainly its silhouette is clearly traced in the opening scenes of Goethe's *Faust*,[9] where Faust, in acute anguish at his inability to satisfy his longings, has reached the point of grasping the cup of poison. His life is saved and his nihilism neutralised by the message of faith and hope that rings out just then in the Easter bells. But his pact with Mephistopheles is a yielding to the devil, the flesh and death, the very elements later identified by Mario Praz as the essence of Romantic agony. That surrender by Faust is actually a substitute for an idealism that has come to fear the spectre of emptiness. Wherever Romantic idealism remained unfulfilled, it threatened to tilt over into agony, as the will to self-transcendence perverted into an urge to self-destruction. Many of the great Romantic heroes attest to this syndrome: Goethe's Werther, Chateaubriand's René, Byron's Don Juan, Musset's Octave, Foscolo's Jacopo Ortis, and most of all, the central figure of the anonymously published *Die Nachtwachen des Bonaventura* (1804). But Romantic agony, though by no means unknown to the early nineteenth century, was still regarded as an inferior alternative, an avowal of failure – the failure of Romantic idealism. It was only the latter half of the century that welcomed the celebration of agony, culminating in so calculated a countersystem as that elaborated in *A Rebours*.

Perhaps Romantic agony was the inevitable nemesis for a transcendental and Utopian idealism that had set its sights too high. Rousseau, Blake, the young Wordsworth, Shelley, Coleridge, Byron, Friedrich Schlegel, Novalis, Wackenroder, Hugo, and Lamartine all subscribed, in one form or another, to the vision of a Golden Age in the future. This Romantic myth assumed varied guises: the innocence of childhood, the goodness of primitive society, harmony with nature, the transformation of the world through poetry. Always the Romantics' impulse was to overreach the present, investing their hopes in a future that fed on the past and on fantasies. But they genuinely and literally believed in the imminent regeneration of the universe, the dawn of a new and better age. Little wonder that they then fell prey to bitter disappointment when these hopes failed to materialise. The very loftiness of the Romantics' ideals predestined them to that disillusionment. In the dangerous extravagance of the Romantics' aims lie the seeds of their unavoidable shortfall, as well as of the ultimate capsizing of their idealism into agony.

Their fine hopes were also severely blighted by the political events of the period. The most damaging blow was that dealt by the French Revolution because it had, at its outset, aroused the highest expectations only to shatter them cruelly in what seemed tantamount to a bankruptcy of humanism. In his sensitive article 'English Romanticism: The Spirit of the Age',[10] M. H. Abrams has shown how the vocabulary of 'hope' and 'joy' prompted by revolutionary exaltation was replaced by 'dejection', 'despair' and 'despondency' when the era of *liberté*, *égalité* and *fraternité* degenerated into the Reign of Terror. The effect of the Revolution on the younger generation in France is brilliantly evoked in the second chapter of Musset's *La Confession d'un enfant du siècle*. The apocalyptic shudder that shook nineteenth-century Europe found its systematic precipitate in the pessimism of Schopenhauer, whose enormous appeal is a sinister comment on the mood of the period. Huysmans, in his 1903 preface to *A Rebours*, explicitly mentions the impact of Schopenhauer, whom he admits to admiring 'plus que de raison' ('beyond the bounds of reason' – p. 29). With the abandonment of any hope for the future other than the blankness of nirvana, despair became almost the norm, from which the only escape was into the Byzantine regions of Decadent perversion. The acid of nineteenth-century nihilism corroded Romantic idealism to the point where all that remained was its inverted image, indeed its caricature, in Romantic agony.

So Romantic agony delineates 'the crack which runs zig-zag across the front of the House of Usher', to quote Mario Praz's vivid image.[11] Continuing the architectural analogy, Praz admits to having focused his attention on that crack in the house of the nineteenth century 'without troubling about its general architecture'. That general architecture, I would suggest, is to be seen in the context of the century as a whole, and, specifically, in that inversion of Romantic idealism, that marks out the configuration of Romantic agony.

NOTES TO CHAPTER 8

1. F. L. Lucas, *The Decline and Fall of the Romantic Ideal* (Cambridge: Cambridge Univ. Press, 1936) p. 278.
2. Koenraad W. Swart, *The Sense of Decadence in Nineteenth-Century France* (The Hague: Martinus Nijhoff, 1964) p. 168.
3. Alfred E. Carter, *The Idea of Decadence in French Literature 1830–1900* (Toronto: Univ. of Toronto Press, 1958).
4. Friedrich Schlegel, *Gespräch uber die Poesie*, in *Kritische Ausgabe*, vol. ii, ed. Hans Eichner (Paderborn: Schöningh, 1967) p. 335.
5. Joris-Karl Huysmans, *A Rebours* (Paris: Union Générale d'Editions, 1975) p. 27. All subsequent references are to this edition.
6. Novalis, *Die Dichtungen* (Heidelberg: Lambert Schneider, 1953) p. 26. All subsequent references are to this edition.
7. Robert Adams, *Nil. Episodes in the Literary conquest of void during the nineteenth century* (London and New York: Oxford Univ. Press, 1966).
8. Carter, *The Idea of Decadence*, p. 151.
9. These scenes already form part of the *Urfaust* fragment, and thus date back to the early 1770s.
10. M. H. Abrams, 'English Romanticism: The Spirit of the Age', in *Romanticism Reconsidered*, ed. Northrop Frye (New York and London: Columbia Univ. Press, 1963) pp. 26–72.
11. Praz, *Romantic Agony*, p. xi.

9 Kafka and the Romantic Imagination

The 'pathetic plight of critics in the face of Kafka's novels'[1] is a matter of notoriety. When *Der Prozess (The Trial)* became available to a large readership in the post-war years, the response was, as Beissner so vividly recalls, one of utter bewilderment ('Ratlosigkeit').[2] The novel was rumoured to be a satire on the Austro-Hungarian monarchy's corrupt bureaucracy and/or a sophisticated allegory of a vaguely religious nature. Neither of these descriptions was at all adequate to the multiple possibilities of interpretation implicit in the work. The perplexity of Kafka's writing has continued to intrigue, challenge and provoke his readers, as is shown by the vast amount of criticism that has appeared in the past thirty years. The bibliography compiled by Harry Järv in 1961 (*Die Kafka Literatur*, Malmo: Bo Cavefors) already comprised over five thousand items; the more recent one by Angel Flores (*A Kafka Bibliography, 1908–1976*. New York: Gordain Press, 1976) lists a profusion of further works.

While most of the criticism has been directed towards an exegesis of the texts, various attempts have also been made to site Kafka within the context of European literature. Psychologically this may represent a defence mechanism on the reader's part. The shock effect is, to some extent at least, defused if Kafka can be assimilated to a tradition; that is, if it can be shown that his works are not so unique as to be literally beyond compare, beyond our previous literary experience.

Many of the suggested comparisons have been with contemporaries or near-contemporaries of his: Camus, Sartre, Gide, Broch, Musil, Benn, Beckett, T. S. Eliot, Rex Warner, Ionesco, Pinter, Silone, and D. H. Lawrence. Among nineteenth-century writers attention has naturally centred on those who attracted Kafka's own interest, namely Flaubert, Dostoyevsky, Gogol,

Strindberg, Kierkegaard, Grillparzer, Hebbel, and above all, Kleist. The parallelism with Kleist is indeed remarkable. It extends far beyond the biographical analogy, the crises of identity and the persistent 'infantilism', as Max Brod termed it.[3] Almost as an afterthought, Brod added that Kafka had consciously schooled his prose on Kleist's. The compact, taut, coldly distanced style is, in fact, only one of several resemblances between them. The most striking feature of both these writers is the discongruity between what is said and the way it is said. In a detached, dispassionate, at times legally dry manner, Kleist and Kafka tell of the disruption and destruction of human life by forces beyond man's control or comprehension. The catastrophe is gratuitous; comment, explanation, and therefore comfort are absent. *Contingit*: an earthquake shatters Chile; Gregor Samsa turns into a beetle. The Marquise of O has to advertise in the newspaper for her child's father; Georg Bendemann has to drown himself. Michael Kohlhaas and K are victims of a faceless and insidious court. Kleist, with his sombre vision of an incomprehensible universe presented in perfectly controlled prose, is Kafka's most obvious literary ancestor. And it is no coincidence that Kafka's deepest kinship should have been to a writer who himself stood outside the mainstream currents of his age, an individualist rejected by Goethe with a shudder of horror.

The search for Kafka's antecedents has rarely gone further back than Kleist, perhaps because Kafka's work is generally perceived as a reflection of the anguish of twentieth-century man. Yet there are significant affinities between Kafka and the Romantics. This topic has attracted surprisingly little attention so far. Dieter Hasselblatt, in his *Zauber und Logik: Eine Kafka Studie* (Köln: Wissenschaft und Politik, 1964, p. 115ff.), articulated the parallel between Kafka and Eichendorff in their common perception of the poetic word as a magical cipher. Jürgen Born went on to explore this area more fully in his article '"Das Feuer zusammenhängender Stunden": Zu Kafkas Metaphorik des dichterischen Schaffens',[4] in which he has collated Kafka's statements about his creative processes with those of the Romantics, notably Eichendorff and E. T. A. Hoffmann. Besides the magical function of the poetic word and the conception of writing as a precipitate of inspiration, Born discerns a number of major similarities between Kafka and the Romantics: the focus on the unconscious and dream, the religious sense, the immanence of the spiritual in the physical, and the consequent predominance of fantasy over empiricism. Heinz Politzer too traces distinctly Romantic features in Kafka in his essay 'Franz Kafkas vollendeter Roman: Zur Typologie seiner Briefe an Felice Bauer'.[5] Politzer's approach is mainly biographical; he suggests that Felice Bauer was in Kafka's life the equivalent of the 'ferne Geliebte' ('the distant beloved') of Eichendorff, Novalis, Hölderlin and Wagner, and that his letters to her are documents of a characteristically Romantic attitude: 'Literatur als Fluch, Kunst als das Kainszeichen des Wahnsinns, der Dichter als Fremder auf den gleichgültigen Landstrassen der Welt, dies ist die Chiffre, in die Kafkas Briefe an Felice zusammenschiessen, eine im Grunde romantische Chiffre' ('Literature as curse, art as the mark of Cain denoting madness, the poet as a stranger on the indifferent highways of the world, that is the emblem that figures over Kafka's letters to Felice, and it is a fundamentally Romantic emblem' – p. 207). These studies are, however, exceptions; the majority of critics, in their emphasis on the 'realism' of Kafka's descriptions and the 'naturalism' of his prose, overlook or even deny any Romantic qualities. Beissner insists that Kafka is 'radikal unromantisch',[6] while to Erich Heller he represents 'the absolute reversal of German idealism'.[7] These judgements are unquestionably true in a certain sense. Yet they spring from a severely delimited vision of Romanticism, from a close and arguably too exclusive association of Romanticism with the cult of beauty and harmony, with idealisation and transcendence. In that respect the term is patently inappropriate to Kafka.

But to envisage Romanticism solely as an escapist Utopianism is a simplification. Its contours extend further to embrace also other facets that were intrinsic to Romanticism from its genesis onwards, and that were increasingly to come to the fore in the course of the nineteenth and twentieth centuries. The awareness of the nocturnal sides of human and organic nature (mooted in Gotthilf Heinrich Schubert's *Ansichten von der Nachtseite der Naturwissenschaften* of 1808), the consciousness of the satanic as well as of the divine forces at work in the world, the fascination with darkness and decay, and with the gruesome as a form of extraordinary beauty: the importance of these aspects of Romanticism must not be underestimated. The inclusion of the outlandish and even the monstrous within the parameter of Romanticism was categorically posited by Friedrich Schlegel in one of his *Athenäum* Fragments (No. 139):

Aus dem romantischen Gesichtspunkt haben auch die Abarten
der Poesie, selbst die exzentrischen und monströsen, ihren
Wert, als Materialien und Vorübungen der Universalität,
wenn nur irgend etwas drin ist, wenn sie nur original sind.

(From the romantic point of view the most curious sorts of
poetry, even the outlandish and the monstrous, are of value as
preliminary exercises to universality, provided there is in them
some grain of originality.)

Victor Hugo was just as emphatic:

la muse moderne verra les choses d'un coup d'oeil plus haut et
plus large. Elle sentira que tout dans la création n'est plus
humainement *beau*, que le laid y existe à côté du beau, le
difforme près du gracieux, le grotesque au revers du sublime,
le mal avec le bien, l'ombre avec la lumière.[8]

(the modern muse will see things with a more lofty and
expansive gaze. She will realise that not everything in creation
is humanly *beautiful*, that the ugly exists alongside the beautiful, the mis-shapen beside the graceful, the grotesque on the
obverse of the sublime, evil with the good, dark with the
light.)

Hugo here uses the word 'modern' – in contrast to primitive and
ancient – to refer to the Christian era, which he equates in one
grandiose sweep with the Romantic age. His observation
becomes even more illuminating when 'modern' is taken in the
more customary and restricted sense to denote the present
century. For one of its dubious distinctions is its open acknowledgement of the inescapability of the ugly, the mis-shapen, the
grotesque, the evil, the monstrous, morally and physically. This
ascendancy of the dystopia over the earlier hopes for Utopia is an
important indication of the significant shift of emphasis in
European Romanticism as it evolved in response to changing
political and cultural conditions.

★   ★   ★   ★   ★

It was by means of the imagination that the Romantic poets
explored the mysterious labyrinths of the universe. As the

primary creative faculty, imagination was invested with an extraordinary range and depth of powers. It was regarded as an 'esemplastic' and transforming force that enabled the poet to perceive the transcendental and to mediate his vision in symbolic images. So imagination became the 'shaping spirit', to quote Coleridge's phrase from his *Dejection Ode*, 'a repetition in the finite mind of the eternal act of creation'.[9] 'It creates anew the universe'[10] in that it portrays not the common reality seen by the mediocre philistine, but the arcane insights of the initiated. The imagination had acquired an absolute and unprecedented autonomy as a corollary to Fichte's creed of subjectivism, whose first command was to heed only unto oneself ('Merke auf dich selbst' are the opening words of the introduction to the *Wissenschaftslehre*). This not only undermined the validity of the external world; it was in fact tantamount to a declaration of the individual's independence of outer phenomena. The world became what the poetic imagination chose to make of it; it existed not in itself, but only as perceived by the poet. There is no better testimony to this than Blake's reply to the question: 'When the Sun rises, do you not see a round disc of fire somewhat like a Guinea?' His answer was: 'O no, no. I see an Innumerable company of the Heavenly host crying, "Holy, Holy, Holy is the Lord God Almighty"'.[11] Just as Blake beheld the heavenly host in the sun, so Kafka saw in Gregor Samsa a beetle. There is, in principle, no difference in the underlying process. In both cases the projection is the outcome of the exercise of the subjective, transforming imagination. What Blake called the 'Corporeal or Vegetative Eye'[12] has been subjugated to the inner eye of the imagination. Significantly, Kafka even used the same image of the eye as Blake. 'Meine Geschichten sind eine Art von Augenschliessen'[13] (literally: 'My stories are a kind of eye-shutting'), he once told Janouch. That phrase is equally apposite to Blake and the visionary company of Romantic poets. They shut their eyes to the outer world, or as Blake put it, they look through it as through a window,[14] in order better to open their eyes to the inner domain which may be beautiful or horrific, a wish- or a fear-image.

By tradition, of course, the Romantic poet was an idealist striving to attain an intuited realm of beauty. Rousseau thought man could be redeemed from the corruption of civilisation; Coleridge and Southey laid plans for a perfect Pantisocratic society; and the German *Frühromantiker* held quite literally that the world could and would gradually be 'poetised'. They believed that the spirit of poetry would progressively transform human life; in this transformation the leader was to be the poet, and the instrument the imagination. Such 'poetisation' is the recurrent theme of Novalis' works. The youth who leaves his home and his beloved in quest of his ideal in *Hyazinth und Rosenblütchen*, a tale interpolated into *Die Lehrlinge zu Saïs*, at last finds the object of his longing, after extensive and arduous travels, in a mysteriously shrouded figure whose veil is lifted to reveal none other than Rosenblütchen herself. The reality of the familiar has been raised to a higher, poetic level, and has assumed a new meaning. The same transfiguration is celebrated in the *Hymnen an die Nacht* and in *Heinrich von Ofterdingen*. The visions that Novalis has at the grave of his beloved become the turning-point of his life for they not only release him from his despair, but also lead to a fundamental reversal of values. Daylight, life, wakefulness are merely to be endured for the sake of night, darkness, sleep and death, which become, through the power of his imagination, gateways into a heaven of consummated beauty that has more substance for him than the world of reality. In *Heinrich von Ofterdingen* this experience is reiterated, though on a less directly personal plane; Heinrich's development as a poet is traced, his initiation into the hallowed kingdom of poetry, and eventually the 'poetisation' of the universe in the symbolical marriage of the seasons with which the novel was to end. It remained a fragment, as did Coleridge's description of his paradise in *Kubla Khan*. Both works were cut short, seemingly by chance: *Heinrich von Ofterdingen* by Novalis' untimely death, and *Kubla Khan* by the disturbance of Coleridge's train of thought – or so he would have us believe. In fact their incompleteness suggests a serious impediment to the fulfilment of the Romantics' aims: the unfeasibility of actually sustaining that transcendence of reality through the imagination to which they aspired.

The shortfall became increasingly apparent with the growing disillusionment of the mid- and later nineteenth century. As the earlier high hopes were dispelled, the Romantic dream tended to turn into nightmare. The 'Beauty of the Medusa', the 'Metamorphoses of Satan', the 'Shadow of the Divine Marquis', 'La Belle Dame sans Merci': these are some of the strands of 'Romantic Agony' analysed by Mario Praz (*The Romantic Agony*, London and New York: Oxford Univ. Press, 1933). These phrases point to some of the paths along which the Romantic imagination encountered the darker sides of life. Images of fear oust the images of hope. Nerval, like Novalis mourning the death of his beloved, is plagued by horrible apparitions of remorse and terror, and only occcasionally is he granted tantalising, intermittent glimpses of the heaven into which Novalis was able to ascend. Instead of the harmonious marriage of the seasons of *Heinrich von Ofterdingen*, a cataclysm of destruction is conjured up in *Aurélia* in 'une scène sanglante d'orgie et de carnage'[15] ('a bloody scene of orgy and carnage') full of monsters, fire, flood, combat, and withered vegetation. Yet this disgusting witches' sabbath is as much a product of the Romantic imagination as Novalis' Elysium. Nor is *Aurélia* an isolated example of the seductive allure of the gruesome for the Romantic imagination. The eerie fate of Coleridge's Ancient Mariner; the insidious snares of malevolent nature that entrap Tieck's characters in such tales as *Der blonde Eckbert* and *Der Runenberg*; the horrific happenings of Mrs Shelley's *Frankenstein*; the precarious dualisms of E. T. A. Hoffmann's world in which the figures are at the mercy of sinister forces beyond their comprehension or control; the shattering perception of the void of nothingness in *Die Nachtwachen des Bonaventura*; the spiritual and physical torments of Rimbaud's *Une Saison en enfer*: these are expressions of the Romantic imagination in despair – despair not just at the realisation that its initial aspirations were unattainable, but that, indeed, human life borders as closely on hell as on heaven. The latitudes of *Aurélia, The Ancient Mariner, Der blonde Eckbert, Frankenstein, Der goldene Topf* and *Une Saison en enfer* are not so far removed from those of *Das Urteil (That Judgement), Die Verwandlung (The Metamorphosis), In der Strafkolonie (In the Penal Colony)* or *Der Prozess (The Trial)*. The modern metamorphosis into the horrendous is the obverse of the Romantic transfiguration into the beautiful. And they are intimately related insofar as both spring from the same source ultimately, from the transforming powers of the imagination.

Nevertheless, there are certain differences, and they should not be minimised. The Romantic poets never lost their consciousness of the inherent duality of the situation; the world of reality, however shadowy, hovers behind that of the imagination. Novalis, for instance, begins his *Hymnen an die Nacht* with a tribute to the splendours of life and light before yielding to the

ecstasies of night; in the second *Hymn*, he returns to the worka-
day round, acknowledging its rights, even though he feels his
true life to be in the visions of darkness. Similarly, Heinrich von
Ofterdingen makes an outer journey to his grandfather in
Augsburg simultaneous with his metaphoric journey to the
realm of poetry. The sub-title 'Délires' of two sections of *Une
Saison en enfer* is an avowal of their hallucinatory character. The
Ancient Mariner has come back from his voyage into the safety
of the harbour and tells his adventures to a wedding-guest, i.e. a
member of the ordinary community. Tieck's Eckbert, like Hoffmann's Anselmus in *Der goldene Topf*, leads a double life in an
apparently orderly, commonplace setting into which the fantastic erupts without warning. To Nerval, 'le Rêve est une second
vie', as he says in the opening phrase of *Aurélia*; the dream is the
second existence, the first being that in reality. For all these
poets, 'die Welt wird Traum, der Traum wird Welt' ('the world
turns into a dream, the dream turns into a world'), to cite the
telling motto for the second part of Novalis' *Heinrich von Ofterdingen*. As the German verb 'wird' (literally: 'becomes') implies,
this is a continuous process. We may watch and follow the
transformation of the world through the imagination, but
always with the knowledge that it is an imaginative transformation from which we may retreat to the safe ground of reality.
When the role of the Ancient Mariner makes excessive demands
on us, we can identify with the wedding-guest.

This is not so with Kafka. Like the Romantics, he drew
extensively on his private visions, as his diaries and his conversations with Janouch show. A diary entry of 6 August 1914 singles
out the 'Sinn für die Darstellung meines traumhaften innern
Lebens'[16] ('the sensibility for the portrayal of my dream-like
inner life') as his paramount concern. Parallels with dreams and
visions punctuate his references to his writing: '*Der Heizer* ist die
Erinnerung an einen Traum'[17] ('*The Stoker* is the memory of a
dream'); '*Das Urteil* ist das Gespenst einer Nacht'[18] ('*The Judgement* is the ghostly vision of one night'); 'Das Schreiben ist eben
eine Art von Geisterbeschwörung'[19] ('writing is a sort of conjura-
tion of spirits'); and when Janouch calls *Die Verwandlung* a
terrible dream, Kafka replies: 'Der Traum enthüllt die
Wirklichkeit'[20] ('the dream reveals the reality'). This is a vital key
to Kafka's stories, and this also is the point at which he differs
from the Romantics. The dream-vision does not stand alongside
reality; the 'real' world, as we experience it, is subsumed into that

of the vision. As a result, it is the starkness of the vision alone that we are left to confront. There is no escape, as from the Romantic realm of fantasy, because there is here only *one* world: that of Kafka's subjective, nightmarish perception. The boundaries between the 'real' and the 'fantastic' have disappeared; Kafka's stories are wholly 'Délires', but these hallucinations are presented as the sole possibility.

Kafka's world may well be 'ver-rückt', as Günther Anders[21] has put it with a clever play on the German word *verrückt*, which generally means 'crazy' but which takes on the sense 'moved out of joint' when the participle is separated by a hyphen. Yet this 'ver-rückt' world is the only one that exists in Kafka's works. Even where there is, for a time, a semblance of ordinariness, as at the beginning of *Das Urteil*, it is soon invaded and overrun by the irrational, which has inescapable validity. Georg Bendemann drowns himself; Gregor Samsa *is* a beetle. It is not a simile, hardly even a metaphor or a symbol; it simply is unavoidably so. This is a clear instance of what Ortega y Gasset has called 'inversion' in modern art: 'before, reality was overlaid with metaphors by way of ornamentation; now the tendency is to eliminate the extrapoetical, or real, prop and to "realize" the metaphor, to make it the *res poetica*'.[22] It is this that Kafka does, and it is this that makes his writings so disconcerting. In the fate of George Bendemann and Gregor Samsa the imaginative transformation has taken place; it is irrevocable, and what faces us is the image of the metamorphosed alone.

The directness of the confrontation causes the shock effect that is so much more intense with Kafka than with the Romantics. The visions leap out at us from Kafka's narratives with an urgency and an immediacy attenuated in the Romantics by the continued presence – even though only in the background – of the world of 'normal' reality. The Romantic realm of the imagination is thus at a certain remove from us. It is remote in another sense too insofar as the other world is often in the past, or in some distant land, or in a mythological setting. Kafka's stories, on the contrary, belong unmistakably to the present; we are acquainted with the houses in which his characters live and the work they do; they seem ordinary people, engrossed in petty problems, worrying and dithering about details. The familiarity of the here and now makes the alienation of his vision all the more disturbing.

This effect is reinforced by the literary representation of the visionary. Herein Kafka's approach is very different to that of the Romantics. They have frequent recourse to the framework or 'window' technique, which in itself leads to a pronounced distancing. Their writing is lofty in manner, with a widespread use of such poetic devices as imagery, repetition, assonance and alliteration. We recognise these as the rhetorical conventions of a poetic style, and from that intellectual cognisance we derive a protective detachment denied to us by Kafka's unadorned directness. His sober, dead-pan, legally precise German brings out the full horror of his visions by giving them concrete substance. A subjective world of fantasy is worked out with such naturalistic circumstantiality, with such unrelenting logic and such a wealth of minute detail that the preposterous hypothesis is endowed with a frightening conviction. The opening paragraph of *Die Verwandlung* is a fine example of Kafka's method:

Als Gregor Samsa eines Morgens aus unruhigen Träumen erwachte, fand er sich in seinem Bett zu einem ungeheueren Ungeziefer verwandelt. Er lag auf seinem panzerartig harten Rücken und sah, wenn er den Kopf ein wenig hob, seinen gewölbten, braunen, von bogenförmigen Versteifungen geteilten Bauch, auf dessen Höhe sich die Bettdecke, zum gänzlichen Niedergleiten bereit, kaum noch erhalten konnte. Seine vielen, im Vergleich zu seinem sonstigen Umfang kläglich dünnen Beine flimmerten ihm hilflos vor den Augen.

(When Gregor Samsa awoke one morning from uneasy dreams, he found himself transformed in his bed into a huge beetle. He was lying on his hard, as it were armour-plated, back and when he lifted his head a little, he could see his dome-like brown belly divided into stiff arched segments on top of which the quilt could hardly keep in position and was about to slide off completely. His numerous legs, which were pitifully thin compared to the rest of his bulk, waved helplessly before his eyes.)

The impact is immediate and violent, and the reader is as little cushioned as Samsa himself against his metamorphosis. There are no shock-absorbers as, for instance, in *The Ancient Mariner*, in which Coleridge deliberately set out to make the extraordinary seem ordinary. But though the Ancient Mariner grasps the wedding-guest 'with his skinny hand' (line 9), the very presence of that wedding-guest as an intermediary between the ghastly tale and the reader acts as an emotional buffer. So do the obvious mythical undertones, the legends of the Flying Dutchman and the Wandering Jew, which facilitate our understanding of Coleridge's poem by allowing us to place it without difficulty in an established lineage. With the transformation of Gregor Samsa into a beetle, we can at best refer to the fairy-tale (*Märchen*) tradition of the prince who has been turned into a frog by some evil spell. That spell is, however, only temporary in the fairy-tale. Whereas in Kafka's stories the magical redeeming word is missing so that they are in effect *Anti-Märchen*.[23] The actuality of the transformation is repeatedly underlined by reminders of the physical condition, such as the rotting apple stuck in Gregor Samsa's back, or the macabre allusion to George Bendemann's athletic prowess in his schooldays as he leaps over the parapet of the bridge. Kafka's stories are indeed 'most wild yet most homely', to use the apt phrase with which the narrator introduces his tale in Edgar Allan Poe's *The Black Cat*. And it is their very homeliness that compels us to accept the truths of their wildness.

A 'literal realist of imagination':[24] that vivid term was coined by Yeats to describe Blake. It is even more fitting to Kafka. The Romantics saw the possibility of a world transformed by the creative imagination; Kafka confronts us with the reality of the accomplished transformation. That the elevation into beauty envisaged by the Romantics in fact abutted on a reduction into the monstrous is the major ironical – and tragic – paradox immanent in European Romanticism.

NOTES TO CHAPTER 9

1. Erich Heller, *The Disinherited Mind* (Harmondsworth: Penguin Books, 1961) p. 177.
2. Friedrich Beissner, *Kafka der Dichter* (Stuttgart: Kohlhammer, 1958) p. 9.
3. Max Brod, 'Infantilismus: Kleist und Kafka', *Die Literarische Welt*, xxviii (15 July 1927) 3–4; Max Brod, *Franz Kafka. Eine Biographie* (New York: Schocken, 1946) pp. 49–52. For further studies of the Kleist-Kafka parallel, see also the following: Heinz Friedrich, 'Heinrich von Kleist und Franz Kafka', *Berliner Hefte für geistiges Leben*, xi (1949) 440–8; John Martin Grandin, 'Existentialist situations in the narrative prose of Franz Kafka and

Heinrich von Kleist', Diss. Michigan, 1970–71; Rainer Grünter, 'Beitrag zur Kafka-Deutung', *Merkur*, xxv, Nr. 3 (1950) 278–87; Franz Hebel, 'Kafka: *Zur Frage der Gesetze* und Kleist: *Michael Kohlhaas', Die Pädagogische Provinz*, x, Nr. 12 (December 1956), 632–8; Helmut Lamprecht, 'Mühe und Kunst des Anfangs. Ein Versuch über Kafka und Kleist', *Neue Deutsche Hefte*, lxvi (1960) 935–40; J. M. Lindsay, 'Kohlhaas and K. Two Men in Search of Justice', *German Life and Letters*, xiii (1959–60) 190–4; F. G. Peters, 'Kafka and Kleist. A Literary Relationship', in *Oxford German Studies*, i (1966) pp. 114–62; Hermann Pongs, 'Kleist und Kafka', *Welt und Wort*, xi (1952) 379–80.

4. Jürgen Born, '"Das Feuer zusammenhängender Stunden": Zu Kafkas Metaphorik des dichterischen Schaffens', in *Das Nachleben der Romantik in der modernen deutschen Literatur*, ed. Wolfgang Paulsen (Heidelberg: Lothar Stiehm, 1969) pp. 177–91.

5. Heinz Politzer, 'Franz Kafkas vollendeter Roman: Zur Typologie seiner Briefe an Felice Bauer', in *Das Nachleben der Romantik in der modernen deutschen Literatur*, ed. Wolfgang Paulsen (Heidelberg: Lothar Stiehm, 1969) pp. 177–91.

6. Beissner, *Kafka der Dichter*, p. 25.

7. Heller, *The Disinherited Mind*, p. 192.

8. Victor Hugo, *Préface de 'Cromwell'* (Paris: Garnier-Flammarion, 1969) p. 69. Italics are Hugo's.

9. Samuel Taylor Coleridge, *Biographia Literaria*, ed. J. Shawcross (Oxford: Clarendon Press, 1907) vol. i, p. 202.

10. Percy Bysshe Shelley, *A Defence of Poetry*, in *Complete Works*, ed. Roger Ingpen and Walter E. Peck (London: Benn, 1965) vol. vii, p. 137.

11. William Blake, *Vision of the Last Judgement*, in *Poetry and Prose*, ed. Geoffrey Keynes (London: Oxford Univ. Press, 1946) p. 651. All subsequent references are to this edition.

12. Blake, *Poetry and Prose*, p. 617.

13. Gustav Janouch, *Gespräche mit Kafka* (Frankfurt: Fischer, 1951) p. 25.

14. Blake, *Poetry and Prose*, p. 617.

15. Gérard de Nerval, *Oeuvres*, ed. Albert Béguin and Jean Richer (Paris: Gallimard, 1952) vol. i, p. 379.

16. Franz Kafka, *Tagebücher* (New York: Schocken, 1951) p. 420.

17. Janouch, *Gespräche mit Kafka*, p. 24.

18. Janouch, *Gespräche mit Kafka*, p. 25.

19. Janouch, *Gespräche mit Kafka*, p. 29.

20. Janouch, *Gespräche mit Kafka*, p. 27.

21. Günther Anders, *Franz Kafka – Pro und Contra* (Munich: Beck, 1951) p. 9.

22. Jose Ortega y Gasset, *The Dehumanization of Art*, trans. Helene Weyl (Princeton: Princeton Univ. Press, 1948) pp. 36–7.

23. Clemens Heselhaus, 'Kafkas Erzählformen', *Deutsche Vierteljahrschrift*, xxvi, Nr. 3 (1952) 353–76.

24. W. B. Yeats, *Essays and Introductions* (New York: Macmillan, 1961) p. 119.

Index

153